SANCTUARIES

Sanctuaries

A Guide to Lodgings in Monasteries, Abbeys, and Retreats of the United States

The Northeast

Jack and Marcia Kelly

Bell Tower New York

A percentage of the royalties from this book will go to the Seva Foundation (Dept. H, 108 Spring Lake Drive, Chelsea, MI 48118) to help fund its worldwide program of compassionate action.

Design by Iris Weinstein.
Drawings by Jennifer Harper from photographs by Jack Kelly.
Maps by Jennifer Harper.
Published by Bell Tower, an imprint of Harmony Books, 201 East 50th Street, New York, New York, 10022. Member of the Crown Publishing Group.
Harmony and colophon and Bell Tower and colophon are trademarks of Crown Publishers, Inc.
Manufactured in the United States of America

Library of Congress Cataloging-in-Publication Data

Kelly, Jack, 1934–
Sanctuaries : a guide to monasteries, abbeys, and retreats in the Northeastern U.S. / Jack and Marcia Kelly. — 1st ed.
p. cm.
Includes index.
1. Monasteries—Guest accommodations—Northeastern States—Directories. 2. Abbeys—Northeastern States—Directories. 3. Retreats—Northeastern States—Directories. I. Kelly, Marcia. II. Title.
BL2527.N7K44 1990
291.6'57'02574—dc20
90-46845
CIP

ISBN 0-517-57727-5

For Gladys Lax Marcus

And in the beginning was love. Love made a sphere: all things grew within it; the sphere then encompassed beginnings and endings, beginning and end. Love had a compass whose whirling dance traced out a sphere of love in the void: in the center thereof rose a fountain.

The Circus of the Sun

ROBERT LAX

Contents

Introduction xi

CONNECTICUT 3

Abbey of Regina Laudis, Bethlehem 4

Benedictine Grange, West Redding 6

Mercy Center, Madison 8

Montfort Retreat Center, Litchfield 10

Oratory of the Little Way, Gaylordsville 12

Vikingsborg Guest House/Convent of St. Birgitta, Darien 14

Villa Maria Retreat House, Stamford 16

Visitation Center, Ridgefield 18

Wisdom House, Litchfield 20

Other Places 23

MAINE 25

Bay View Villa, Saco 26

China Lake Conference Center, China 28

Ferry Beach Park Association, Saco 30

Goose Cove Lodge, Sunset 32

Hersey Retreat, Stockton Springs 34

Marie Joseph Spiritual Center, Biddeford 36

Notre Dame Spiritual Center, Alfred 38

St. Joseph-by-the-Sea, Peaks Island 40

Other Places 43

MASSACHUSETTS 45
Eastern Point Retreat House, Gloucester 46
Emery House, West Newbury 48
Glastonbury Abbey, Hingham 50
Insight Meditation Society, Barre 52
Kripalu Center for Yoga and Health, Lenox 54
Miramar Retreat Center, Duxbury 56
Mount Carmel Retreat House, Williamstown 58
Mount St. Mary's Abbey, Wrentham 60
Sacred Heart Retreat House, Ipswich 62
St. Benedict Priory, Still River 64
St. Joseph's Abbey, Spencer 66
St. Stephen Priory Spiritual Life Center, Dover 68
Other Places 71

NEW HAMPSHIRE 75
Aryaloka, Newmarket 76
The Common, Peterborough 78
Durham Retreat Center, Durham 80
Hundred Acres Monastery, New Boston 82
St. Anselm Abbey/Manchester Priory, Manchester 84
St. Francis Retreat Center, Rye Beach 86
Star Island, Isle of Shoals 88
Other Places 91

NEW JERSEY 93
Good Shepherd Center, Morristown 94
Loyola House of Retreats, Morristown 96
St. Marguerite's Retreat House, Mendham 98
St. Mary's Abbey–Delbarton, Morristown 100
St. Paul's Abbey/Queen of Peace Retreat House, Newton 102
Villa Pauline, Mendham 104
Other Places 107

NEW YORK 110
Abba House of Prayer, Albany 112
Abbey of the Genesee, Piffard 114
Abode of the Message, New Lebanon 116
The Chaleight, Wells 118
Chapel House, Hamilton 120
Chautauqua Institution, Chautauqua 122
Chrysalis House, Warwick 124
Cormaria Center/St. Mark's House of Prayer, Sag Harbor 126
Dai Bosatsu Zendo, Livingston Manor 128
Holy Cross Monastery, West Park 130
Holy Trinity Community, Hornell 132
House of the Redeemer, New York 134
Jesuit Retreat House, Auriesville 136
Linwood Spiritual Center, Rhinebeck 138
Marian Shrine, West Haverstraw 140
Mount Irenaeus Franciscan Mountain Retreat, West Clarksville 142
Mount St. Alphonsus Spiritcare Center, Esopus 144
Mount St. Francis Hermitage, Maine 146
Mount Saviour Monastery, Pine City 147
New Skete Communities, Cambridge 150
Our Lady of the Resurrection Monastery, La Grangeville 152
Our Lady's Guest and Retreat House/Graymoor, Garrison 154
The Priory, Chestertown 156
St. Cuthbert's Retreat House, Brewster 158
St. Francis Center, Oyster Bay 160
St. Gabriel's Retreat House, Shelter Island 162
St. Joseph Spiritual Life Center, Valatie 164
St. Mary's Villa, Sloatsburg 166
Springwater Center, Springwater 168
Still Point House of Prayer, Stillwater 170
Transfiguration Monastery, Windsor 172
Wellsprings, Glens Falls 174
Zen Mountain Monastery, Mount Tremper 176
Other Places 179

PENNSYLVANIA 185
Daylesford Abbey, Paoli 186
Dominican Retreat House, Elkins Park 188
Pendle Hill, Wallingford 190
Rosemont Spiritual Center, Rosemont 192
St. Joseph's-in-the-Hills Retreat House, Malvern 194
St. Raphaela Mary Retreat House, Haverford 196
Other Places 199

RHODE ISLAND 203
Mercy Lodge, Cumberland 204
Mount St. Joseph Spiritual Life Center, Bristol 206
Nazareth Center, Newport 208
Our Lady of Peace Spiritual Life Center, Narragansett 210
Portsmouth Abbey, Portsmouth 212
Providence Zen Center, Cumberland 214
St. Paul's Priory Guest House, Newport 216
Other Places 219

VERMONT 221
Karmê-Chöling, Barnet 222
Milarepa Center, Barnet 224
Monastery of the Immaculate Heart of Mary, Westfield 226
Weston Priory, Weston 228
Other Places 231

Glossary 233

Index 235

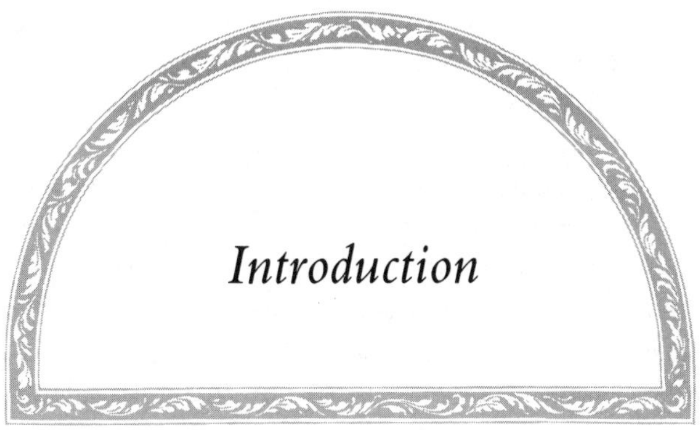

Introduction

These places—monasteries, abbeys, retreats—are a world apart, in which time as we know it is suspended. Those who have chosen to live in these places are devoting themselves wholeheartedly, and with as much singleness of purpose as they can muster, to understanding what it means to be a human being. This atmosphere allows visitors to reflect in unaccustomed solitude.

In this introduction, we would like to share some of the basics that will help you appreciate the rhythms of monastic life, and make your journeys as fulfilling as ours have been:

Philosophy As you will see, we have visited everything from Trappist monasteries to Buddhist temples, and at each place the message has been the same: "We welcome people of all faiths." The visitor is invited to join in any services that the community holds, but in most places there is no requirement to do so. (Those that request guests to join them in prayer are so noted.)

Purpose Monasteries and abbeys are usually functioning religious communities that have some rooms for visitors, while the purpose of retreat houses is to provide a setting for groups to hold meetings or retreats. There are often rooms available for individuals (private retreatants) even when a group retreat is going on. Individuals can sometimes join in the group sessions, and can always join in prayer services. It is important to remember that the people who live in these places are not prepared to do psychological counseling, so don't make such a retreat if that is your expectation or need.

Settings and accommodations We visited everything from exquisite mansions on the shore to simple cabins in the woods. We left every one of them feeling happy, rested, and at peace, in large part because of the spirit of those who live there. Accommodations ranged from spacious rooms with a private bath and a view to monks' cells with dormitory bathrooms. Early in our travels, when on one occasion we were led up a dark stairway, we began to worry. However, our fears were unfounded, and this place, like the others, was wonderful, and refreshed our spirits.

Some places have hermitages, usually for one person who wants to be alone, occasionally for two. Although many of the buildings were once houses of the very rich, the accommodations are generally plain and simple, yet comfortable and clean. Most places welcome men, women, and children. Any variations are noted in the text. You should not bring pets with you, but you will encounter resident dogs and cats from time to time.

Costs One center, in its brochure, sums up the financial story very well for all those we have visited: "We try to keep our fees moderate; however, they do not cover all our expenses. Supplemental donations can help us maintain our center. We are grateful for your generous support. Financial arrangements are negotiable if the fee is a burden." As you will see in our listings, 1989–1990 prices run from $12 to $50 a night. By the time you read this book, the prices may have risen slightly. Unless otherwise stated, fees *include* three meals a day, so whatever extra you can afford is a gift in the true sense of the word.

Customs, comportment, attire "Turning the bed," or making your bed with fresh sheets before you leave, is an accepted practice in this world. In some places, guests are expected to pitch in and help with chores (this is always noted in the text); in others, the staff prefer no help at all. Work on the property, with the community, is usually available if you request it.

Courtesy and sensitivity to others is the general rule. Guests and community are there for quiet and contemplation, so radios, typewriters, and chatting in the hallways or chapel will only be disturbing. Following the lead of the community in chapel or meditation will easily carry you through any local customs.

Attire can be casual, though it should be respectful. Many in the religious communities wear work shirts and jeans except when in chapel, though guests may even dress casually there. It was impossible to identify the man in the straw hat and overalls as the abbot during a recent monastery sheep-shearing weekend!

Reservations It is essential to make reservations at each of these places. Some are booked weeks or months ahead on weekends, particularly for groups. Individuals can often get a bed with less notice, and weekdays are easier for all. In any case, do not appear without having called ahead. If you request a brochure with details about a particular place, this will be mailed to you.

Transportation To help orient you geographically, we have included driving directions, but some places are very hard to find, so be prepared for some wrong turns. Most places have directions in their brochures for arrival by car or public transportation. Many can arrange to meet you at the airport or station.

Other places At the end of each section, there is a list of additional monasteries, abbeys, and retreats that were recommended to us, but that we have not yet visited. In order to ensure that you write ahead, some places do not give out their phone numbers.

What a journey this has been! We began as two travelers, pleased to discover new and marvelous places to stay. By the end we realized that the grandest estates and the simplest retreat houses brought us equal delight. Although we had not started out with a religious intent, we often joined the community we were visiting for prayer or meditation, and grew to appreciate the deep measure of rest and renewal available, no matter what the form.

We have tried to impart the feeling of each place we visited, to help you decide whether you prefer a weekend of complete silence near the sea, a hermitage retreat in the mountains, nine days of sitting zazen, or a stay in a cheerful island community. The range is tremendous, but the spirit is consistent.

As you begin your travels, we would like to share with you this Irish blessing, which we found at St. Benedict Priory, Still River, Massachusetts:

May the road rise to meet you.
May the wind be always at your back.
May the sun shine warm upon your face,
The rains fall soft upon your fields,
And until we meet again, may God
Hold you in the palm of His hand.

Jack and Marcia Kelly

NEW YORK CITY

SANCTUARIES

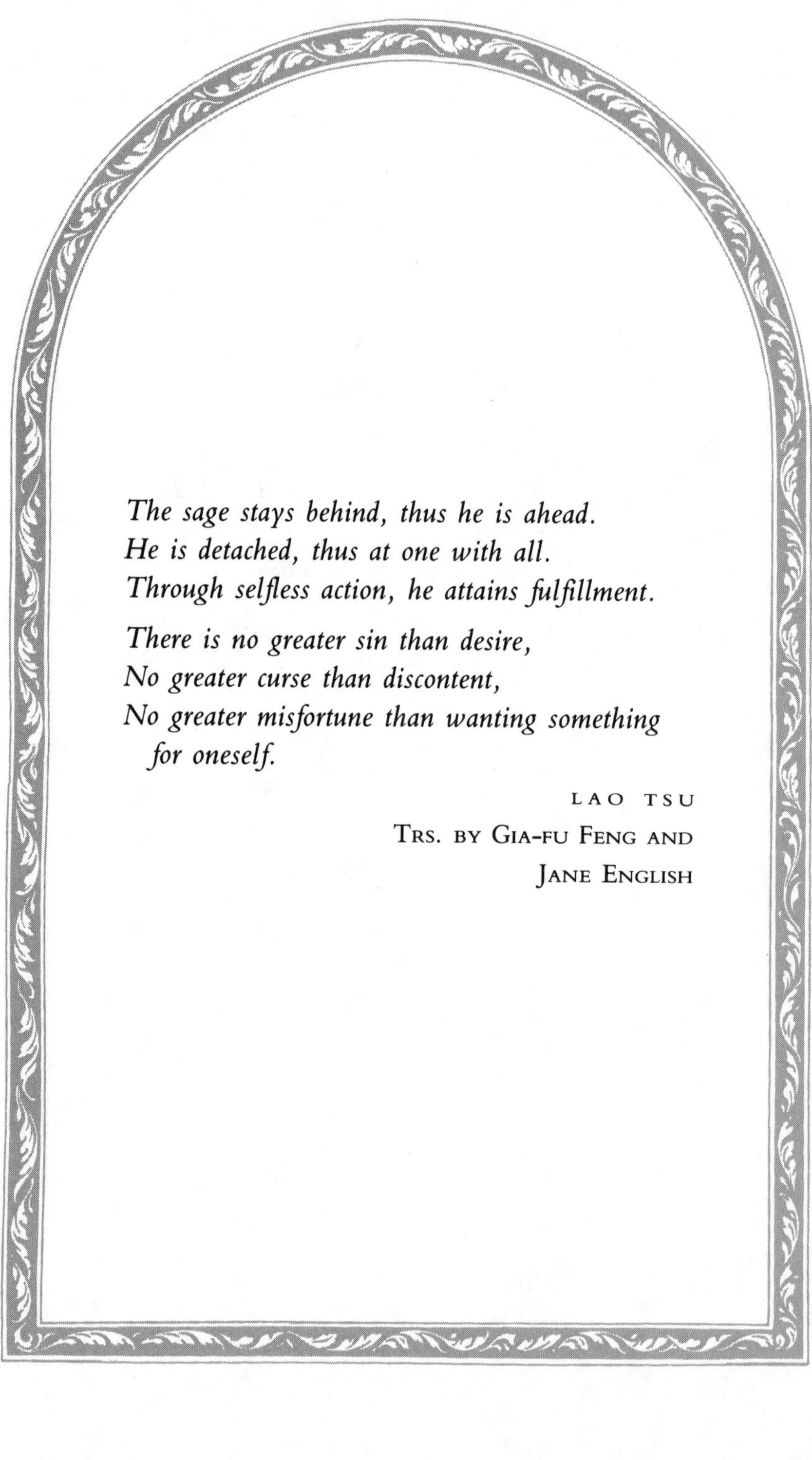

The sage stays behind, thus he is ahead.
He is detached, thus at one with all.
Through selfless action, he attains fulfillment.

There is no greater sin than desire,
No greater curse than discontent,
No greater misfortune than wanting something
for oneself.

LAO TSU

TRS. BY GIA-FU FENG AND
JANE ENGLISH

Connecticut

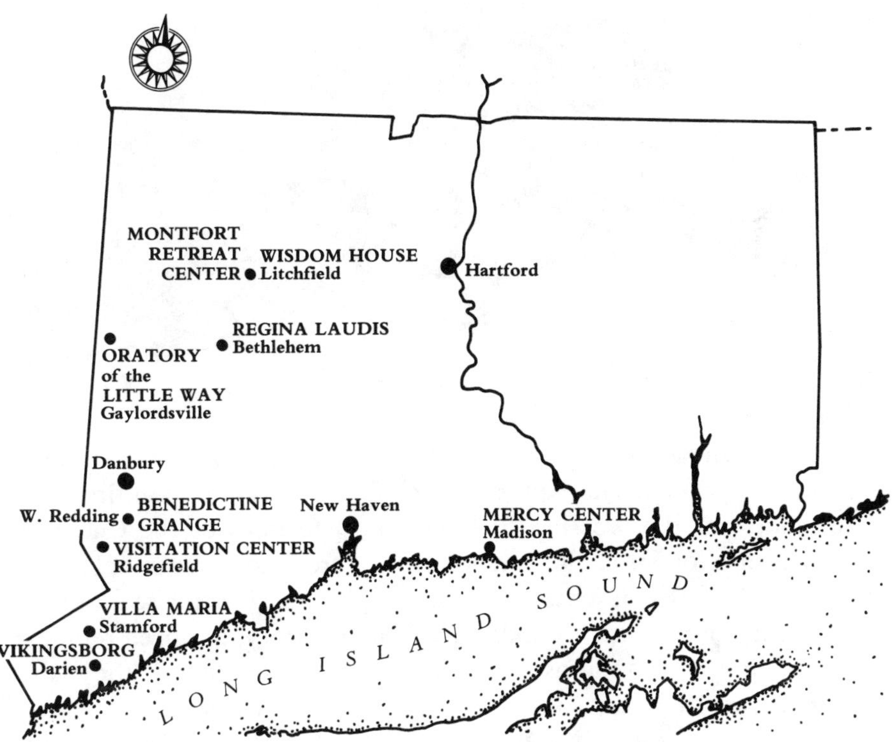

Abbey of Regina Laudis
Bethlehem, CT

The original land for this monastery was donated by an industrialist from Waterbury who felt that the hilltop was too beautiful for anything but the worship of God. In 1946, nuns of the Catholic Benedictines of Strict Observance arrived from the French abbey of Jouarre and settled in what is now St. Joseph's, the guesthouse for men.

The main monastery building, a former factory, has been remodeled to house the 50 nuns. Surrounded by wooden fences, the main building is off limits to all guests, except the entrance, the guest refectory, and the wood-paneled chapel that is connected to the convent. Here the nuns gather seven times a day, between 6:45 A.M. and 8 P.M., and once at night at 2 A.M., to sing the Hours of the Divine Office. Mass in Gregorian chant is sung every day at 7:45 A.M. The nuns sit behind a screen, the curtain parted for most services so the habited singers can be glimpsed through the latticework.

The guesthouses are austere—reminiscent of a working farm—but clean and sensible, with great attention to whatever is needed. St. Joseph's, with its single, sparsely furnished rooms for men only, with a bed, writing table, and chair, and community bath, is like a French farmhouse. The main living-dining area is dominated by a stone fireplace, with windows on either side that give balance and light to the dark wood walls.

St. Gregory's, the women's guesthouse (an authentic 1794 New

England farmhouse), is decorated in soft, pale colors. Women take their meals in the monastery in a separate refectory from the nuns. Men's meals are brought to St. Joseph's and served by one of the nuns. The monastery is a working farm with dairy cows that provide fresh milk that the nuns make into butter and cheese. They also bake their own bread, and the food is excellent.

There are no organized retreats, but hospitality is a very important part of the life here. A nun is assigned to talk with each visitor as the need arises. The monastery makes no distinction as to race or creed, but those who come should be willing to observe the monastic life-style. The nuns are rooted in the ancient Benedictine monastic ways, but are still flexible to the future. "Come to find peace of mind," one suggested, "and the strength of a spiritual existence."

The monastery grounds comprise 300 acres, most of it used for farming. There is a separate building that houses an 18th-century Neapolitan créche. The elegant figures depict individual attitudes toward the infant Jesus, from devotion and love to indifference. It is fitting that this nativity scene should be a major point of interest on the grounds of a monastery in a place called Bethlehem.

Abbey of Regina Laudis
Box 273, Flanders Rd.
***Bethlehem, CT** 06751*
(203) 266-7724

Accommodations: *10 small singles for men in the men's guesthouse, and up to 9 women in doubles and triples in the women's guesthouse; delicious home-cooked meals (men and women dine separately); canonical hours, mass in Latin; meeting with community member and work on property suggested; first Friday and Saturday in August is the annual fair; open year-round, though guests are discouraged during Lent; free-will donations help the community. Write to the Guest Secretary with reason for coming and alternate dates.*

Directions: *From I-84 East, at Exit 15, take U.S. 6 through Woodbury. Turn left onto Flanders Rd., where there is a sign for the abbey. In 4 miles, the entrance to the abbey is on your right.*

From I-84 West, at Exit 17, take Rte. 64 through Middlebury. Turn right onto U.S. 6 in Woodbury, then proceed as above.

From the north, take Rte. 63 in Litchfield. Turn right onto Rte. 61 through Bethlehem; at the cemetery, bear right and then turn left onto Flanders Rd. The abbey is 1 mile farther, on your left.

Benedictine Grange
West Redding, CT

Set on 15 acres of suburban land in a typical old Connecticut neighborhood, the Benedictine Grange is described as an experiment in contemporary monastic living, combining the ancient traditions of Saint Benedict, who espoused the concept of prayer and work, with the needs of serving the community where one lives. Father John Giuliani, a Roman Catholic priest who had spent almost a decade as chaplain at Sacred Heart University in Bridgeport, felt the need for a more reflective life. With the blessing of his bishop, Father John purchased this land in 1977 and began a new phase on his spiritual path.

The Grange, named after granaries used by early Benedictine monks for shelter and prayer following work in the fields, acquired a pre–Civil War barn and dismantled and reassembled it for use as the main place of worship. Every Sunday at 10:30 A.M., more than a hundred people come for mass to the accompaniment of guitars, soft drums, and specially composed music. Father John breaks loaves of freshly baked bread for the communion. This celebration has a true sense of community and spiritual cohesiveness. There is great support for the charitable activities of the Grange, which operates a soup kitchen in Norwalk, providing meals for more than 100 people each day. Through the 1980s, its Quest for Peace Program sent millions of dollars' worth of goods to the poor in Latin America.

Just a five-minute drive from the Grange there is a recently acquired guest house that has six beds. One of the dreams of Father John was to have a dwelling for guests called Mary's House. Associates of the Grange investigated a house that looked promising, and discovered a relief depiction of Mary with the infant Jesus as part of the stonework in the living-room fireplace. When Father John saw the sculpture, he said, "This is it." The beautifully reconditioned house, like the Grange and its grounds, reflects the taste and touch of Father John, who is in every sense an artist. Those who would visit are asked to write ahead to allow proper preparation. Guests are expected to structure their own time. There are morning and evening prayer services at 7 A.M. and 5:30 P.M., four times a week, held in a separate meditation room near the main chapel at the Grange. "Many wounded persons find their way here," Father John said, "and we reach out in our own way to comfort with the gospel, pure and simple."

The Grange also runs St. Benedict's Guild—a wonderful shop in the old railroad station at Cannondale—offering art, sacred artifacts, and ethnic crafts, mainly from Third World countries.

Benedictine Grange
Mary House
48 Beeholm Rd.
West Redding, CT *06896*

Accommodations: *3 rooms for 6 men and women; gourmet dinner with resident couple; food may be brought and kept in refrigerator for breakfast and lunch; morning and evening prayer at the Grange, Thursday through Sunday, and a mass on Sunday at 10:30 A.M.; country roads for walking; gardens at Grange; lovely gift shop nearby; open year-round; dependent on free-will donations. Write for reservations in advance, giving alternate dates.*

Directions: *U.S. 7 to Rte. 107 to Beeholm Rd. on right for Mary House, and to Dorethy Rd. on right (a total of 2 miles), for the Grange, on left.*

Mercy Center
Madison, CT

In 1939, W. T. Grant, the founder of the Grant retail chain, bought 38 acres of land with 1,100 feet fronting on Long Island Sound, and built on it an 18-room mansion of brick and California redwood. The property is reported to have two of every tree and bush that can sustain itself in this climate, such as Japanese ginkgo, Chinese pine, Russian olive, and Siberian crabapple. In 1948 the estate was given to the Hartford diocese, and the property became the site for a novitiate house for the Sisters of Mercy. That same year a new wing was added, and a larger addition was built in 1955. The rooms available can now accommodate 104.

After Vatican II, the Sisters of Mercy redirected their programs, and the facility evolved from a novitiate to a spiritual renewal center. Gradually, as the programs grew in scope and attendance, the Mercy Center became an obvious choice for groups looking for a quiet place to hold meetings, attracting civic and corporate groups, and those concerned with human development.

The original rooms of the mansion form the core of this complex, beautifully maintained and comfortably furnished with many private areas to sit in and read. The former living room, with dramatic views of the Sound, is now the chapel. Meals are taken buffet-style in the large dining room.

This is a busy conference center with nine meeting rooms, as well as a lecture hall and auditorium, but the lovely setting on the water gives a feeling of both openness and privacy. A place of natural beauty and hospitality that one guest described as "comfortable as a cup of tea."

Mercy Center
167 ***Neck Rd., Box*** *191*
Madison, CT *06443*
(203) 245-0401

Accommodations: *Beds for 104 men and women in singles and doubles; buffet-style meals in a 110-seat dining room; chapel; reading rooms, porches, patios; 38 acres, beach overlooking Long Island Sound; open year-round; $49 and up a night.*

Directions: *From I-95N, take Exit 59. Turn right off the exit, then left at the traffic light onto Rte. 1; two miles along Rte. 1 (right after Mobil gas station) turn right onto Neck Rd. About 1/2 mile on the left, you will see the sign for Mercy Center.*

Montfort Retreat Center
Litchfield, CT

The Catholic Montfort Missionaries acquired this property in 1947, the year their founder, Louis de Montfort, was canonized a saint. Originally used as a seminary, the stone mansion was turned into a retreat center in the late 1960s. The house and its annex stand on a hilltop facing south, with 170 acres of woods and fields.

Inside the main entrance, to the right, is the chapel where mass is said every day. The priests make the center available to groups or individuals seeking a place and time for prayer and devotion. There are 35 beds available in 25 rooms with semiprivate baths.

In 1958 the priests and brothers built a grotto here, modeled after  Our Lady of Lourdes in France, calling it Lourdes of Litchfield. The 35 acres of shrine grounds are open year-round. Devotion services and pilgrimage programs are held outside from early May to mid-October. There is an outstanding Way of the Cross that ascends to the Crucifixion scene.

In addition to the Lourdes grotto, there are separate shrines to the Sacred Heart, Saint Michael, Saint Jude, Saint Joseph, and Saint Louis de Montfort. Thousands of pilgrims have come to visit here each year.

The great stone retreat center, standing above and apart from the shrines, offers a separate place for spiritual sustenance.

Montfort Retreat Center
***P.O. Box** 667*
***Litchfield, CT** 06759*
(203) 567-8434

Accommodations: *Singles and doubles for 35 men and women; buffet-style meals; chapel and shrine open daily; 170 hilltop acres; open year-round; $34.50 a night.*

Directions: *From I-95, take Exit 27A (Rte. 8/Waterbury). Follow Rte. 8 North through Waterbury to Exit 42 (Rte. 118/Litchfield). Turn left and take Rte. 118 West for 5 miles. The entrance to the center is on Rte. 118 before you reach the center of town, and is marked on your right by an entrance sign to* LOURDES IN LITCHFIELD.

Oratory of the Little Way

Gaylordsville, CT

Named in honor of Saint Thérèse of Lisieux, the Oratory of the Little Way was founded by Episcopalian Father Benjamin Priest. In the late 1960s he was given four acres of land on the outskirts of Gaylordsville, and began to build a country retreat as a memorial to his wife and son. At age 65, after 19 years of service at Trinity Church in Manhattan, in 1971 he moved to this quiet Connecticut neighborhood, not to retire but to continue his religious life in a different way.

With the help of young people he had befriended at the Trinity Church Coffee Shop, he built a modest and comfortable country house that includes a living-dining room, kitchen, chapel, and bedrooms for four visitors. He was joined in the 1980s by an Episcopal nun, and together they offer hospitality to anyone interested in spiritual growth. They follow the example of Saint Thérèse, who taught that holiness consists not in being perfect or heroic, but in living each day in a truly human way.

The informal atmosphere of the place is exemplified by the daily mass Father Priest says at the dining-room table, which he likens to the Last Supper. We were entranced by the simple solemnity of this service.

Father Priest and Sister Mary Michael are available if they are needed—to talk or pray with, and to share meals. The chapel is the focal point of the house—small, distinctive, and very peaceful. "We all try to model ourselves on heroes, and then get upset when we fall short of our ideals," says Father Priest. "God does not create junk. We have to accept the raw material we are given. Accept it for what it is, then we can grow." He quotes the following verse:

Since the more we learn,
The less we know,
Let the child return
And wisdom grow.

Oratory of the Little Way
Box 221, South Kent Rd.
Gaylordsville, CT 06755
(203) 354-8294

Accommodations: *Rooms for 4 men and women; family-style meals in dining room following Eucharist; chapel; pretty grounds and country roads for walking; open year-round; dependent on free-will offerings.*

Directions: *Located 22 miles north of Danbury, and 7 miles north of New Milford. Take U.S. 7 to Gaylordsville; cross the bridge and turn right immediately onto River Rd; take the first left onto South Kent Rd. (at post office and volunteer fire dept.) and go 1/2 mile (past graveyard on left) to Oratory Lane on right; look for a large white house with a red cross on the face of the building and a sign at the entrance to the drive.*

Vikingsborg Guest House Convent of St. Birgitta

Darien, CT

This spacious guesthouse is on a cove of Long Island Sound, in a quiet residential neighborhood. In 1957 the property was donated by Margaret Tjader to the Birgittines, an order of nuns founded by Saint Birgitta of Sweden in the 14th century. Margaret's parents, a Swedish father and an American mother, were missionaries, deeply religious people who made their house available to people of all faiths except Catholics. Margaret, who was curious about all religions, often traveled to Sweden. There she became a friend and admirer of Mother Elisabeth, who was instrumental in the resurgence of the Birgittines in the 20th century. Margaret converted to Catholicism, and donated the beautiful waterfront property to the Catholic nuns who now live here. In her book on the life of Mother Elisabeth, Margaret wrote, "Change is the law of nature, the rhythm of history; the tumult, decline, resurgence, triumph and decline again—the wheel of human life."

The nuns, who still wear religious habits with distinctive white bands securing the veils to their heads like hot-cross buns, have 11 beds available for guests. The furnishings, gathered by the Tjaders during their mission travels, are outstanding, museum-quality pieces.

Meals are served in the grand dining room by the nuns three times a day. One of the wings of the house, the former trophy room, has been converted to a chapel where the nuns gather daily to sing liturgy at 6 A.M., noon, 4 P.M., and 9 P.M. Mass is said Monday through Saturday at 7:30 A.M. and at 8 on Sunday. Guests are welcome.

There is a spacious porch, often used as a meeting room for local groups who come to worship in the chapel and have a meal. The nuns do not give retreats, but make their house available for group meetings, individuals, and couples seeking a quiet, restful place.

The nine-acre abbey grounds, with tall pines and well-tended lawns, have a feeling of substance and continuity. The seawall has stairs where missionaries led their followers into the water to be baptized. There is a small stone chapel, set on a knoll, a former playhouse that has been converted to a place of prayer and contemplation. At night there is a wonderful view to the south, across the water, of the twinkling lights on Long Island.

Vikingsborg Guest House
Convent of St. Birgitta
Tokeneke Trail
Darien, CT 06820
(203) 655-1068

Accommodations: *12 beds in singles and doubles, and a guest cottage for 4; meals served to guests in formal dining room; daily mass and 4 prayer services; woodland walks and gardens; bathing from private dock; open year round; $40 a night.*

Directions: *From I-95 N take Exit 12 and turn right onto Tokeneke Rd. Proceed 1/2 mile on Tokeneke Rd. to an intersection island; bear right around the island to Old Farm Rd.; drive 1/2 mile to Tokeneke Trail. Bear right on Tokeneke Trail and proceed 1/2 mile to Runkenhage Rd. (Note green, shield-shaped sign on left.) Turn onto Runkenhage Rd. to the first driveway on the right (about 50 feet from the turn); drive through two sets of stone posts in the direction of the sign.*

Villa Maria Retreat House

Stamford, CT

Originally owned by a Broadway producer and rented as a writing retreat by Clare Booth Luce, this beautiful, Georgian-style mansion was purchased in 1947 by the Bernadine Sisters for use as a retreat center. These Catholic nuns trace their lineage back to a cloistered community of Bernadine Franciscans who left Poland in 1894 to teach the children of Polish immigrants in Philadelphia. Eventually a group of these nuns came to teach in Stamford, and when the local bishop expressed interest in establishing a retreat house, they complied.

There are 18 acres of landscaped grounds surrounding the retreat center. The great lawns are planted with dogwoods, and one section has a splendid corridor of pines. Nearby, in a rectangular lawn area surrounded by low hedges, are statue depictions of the Stations of the Cross.

In the 1950s, a wing was added to the mansion that has double rooms for 64 retreatants, with a bath for every two rooms. The rooms, hallways, and bath facilities are crisp and clean.

The peaceful chapel is imperceptibly connected to the main house and the retreat rooms by corridors that lead from the original house to the new section. The dining room is staffed by seemingly ageless nuns who embody Bernadine hospitality. The aim of the community is true service, and groups of all denominations are welcome.

The community meets at 6 A.M. for morning prayer, and again at 3:45 P.M. for rosary and at 4 P.M. for evening prayer. A resident chaplain celebrates mass daily at 6:30 A.M. Each Thursday there is a holy hour from 2:30 to 3:30 P.M., with the Holy Eucharist. Retreatants are welcome at all these services.

The estate garage behind the main house is used as a separate prayer house. With its living room, kitchenette, three bedrooms, two baths, and small chapel, it is an ideal place for small group meetings.

A full program of weekend retreats is conducted by the staff, as well as Spiritual Enrichment Programs that are offered as morning or full-day sessions, or ongoing, one-evening-per-week meetings. The intention is to reach out to people, in as many ways as possible, to help them find comfort and peace through prayer.

Villa Maria Retreat House
159 Sky Meadow Dr.
Stamford, CT 06903
(203) 322-0107

Accommodations: *Beds for 64 men and women in singles and doubles, and the prayer house with 3 bedrooms, available for men and women; plain, buffet-style meals in dining room; daily mass, morning and evening prayer; 18 landscaped acres; open year-round; $75 a weekend.*

Directions: *From the Merritt Pkwy., take Exit 35. Turn left onto High Ridge Rd. (Rte. 137 North) and drive about 2 miles, passing the Stamford Museum and Nature Center. Watch for a small green sign on the right reading VILLA MARIA—NEXT LEFT. Turn left on Sky Meadow Dr. At the top of the hill, turn right onto the retreat house driveway. Park in the rear, and enter through the glass-enclosed area.*

Visitation Center
Ridgefield, CT

The Catholic nuns of the Congregation of Notre Dame purchased the 48-acre Lynch estate in 1962 for use as a novitiate house. From 1968 to 1972 the nuns ran a private girls' school in the building now called the Visitation Center. From 1972 to 1985, the center was used for community retreats and meetings, as well as by local groups for lay deacon training and by Presbyterians as a place for worship while their burned church was being rebuilt.

In 1985 the classrooms were converted to double sleeping rooms, and the Congregation of Notre Dame decided to provide a place for those seeking to explore and express the value and dignity of human life. Programs in spirituality are offered for young people, families, the elderly, and the underprivileged.

The nuns encourage youth groups to come here, which is unusual for retreat houses, because young people can be rather lively. This is a great facility for them, high on a hill, with its own grounds to wander on and a building designed for hard knocks. Every other bedroom still has class blackboards on one wall, but the rooms are well furnished, bright, and cheerful. There are large meeting rooms, one set up like a small auditorium with tiered seating and separate chairs with arm desks. There is also a full-size gymnasium. Kitchen facilities are available so that a group can be self-contained, but groups often go down the drive a short distance to take meals in the dining room at the mansion. There is mass in the mansion chapel daily at 11:30 A.M.

There is a splendid meditation room in the center, designed around a triangle shape, the ancient symbol of the Trinity. The room's architecture, benches, glasswork, and tabernacle door reflect this theme. The Blessed Sacrament is kept there.

Down the short drive, past the Lynch mansion and around the convent, is a large open field, kept cut and neat, a great area for walks and outdoor recreation. The views from this gently sloping field to the west and north are quite spectacular, looking over two lakes in New York State, a few miles away, and across the mountains.

Visitation Center
223 ***West Mountain Rd.***
Ridgefield, CT *06877*
(203) 438-9071

Accommodations: *Beds for 51 men and women, mainly doubles; bring own food and use kitchen or have buffet-style meals in mansion dining room; mass daily; lovely meditation room; 48 mountaintop acres; open year-round except for 2 weeks in summer; costs vary.*

Directions: *From Rte. 84, take Exit 3 (Merritt Parkway/Norwalk). Follow U.S. 7 South to Rte. 35 (Amoco gas station is on the right). Take Rte. 35 South to Ridgefield. Once you pass the turn for Rte. 116, count traffic lights. At the second light, turn right onto Catoonah. Follow that to the end. At stop sign, turn right onto High Ridge and make an immediate left at the stop sign onto Barry Ave./West Mountain Rd. Travel 2.3 miles. There is a white sign on the left reading CONGREGATION OF NOTRE DAME—VISITATION CENTER. Follow the driveway to the first intersection; the center is just to the left. Come to the door on the right.*

Wisdom House
Litchfield, CT

The Daughters of Wisdom, an order of Catholic nuns founded in France in 1703 by Marie-Louise Trichet under the spiritual guidance of Saint Louis de Montfort, purchased this property in 1949 for their first American novitiate house. The original farmhouse, built in the 1800s, is used for silent retreats for groups of 20 people. The large brick building, which contains a chapel, dining rooms, conference rooms, and beds for 100, was built in 1953 and used as the Seat of Wisdom College from 1960 to 1965. The four-story building, with elevator access, is clean and well maintained. The rooms are former classrooms and the halls are unconverted school corridors. The beds are comfortable and the rooms well proportioned. There are large, enclosed sitting porches on the second and third levels, with views over the surrounding hills.

The Daughters of Wisdom run a full series of retreats ranging from one-day sessions of Christian yoga to full weekends of Meyer-Briggs workshops, clowning ministry (which teaches silent clowning for use in liturgy), youth work, adult education, and ministry for shut-ins. They also accommodate private retreatants and have ongoing Elderhostel programs.

The 58 acres were once a working farm, and there are miles of good walking country. Less than a mile away is Topsmead, a Connecticut state forest, with wonderful hiking trails.

Wisdom House
*229 **East Litchfield Rd.***
***Litchfield, CT** 06759*
(203) 567-3163

Accommodations: *14 bedrooms in 200-year-old farmhouse; accommodations for 100 men, women, and children in a large brick building; community dining; 58 acres of woods and meadows for cross country skiing and meditation; biking on country roads; forest preserve just up road; swimming pool; Elderhostels; open year-round; $35 a night.*

Directions: *Wisdom House is on the corner of Clark Rd. and East Litchfield Rd., 2 miles west of Exit 42 off Rte. 8 in the East Litchfield section of Litchfield. From Litchfield Center, take Rte. 118 East 2 3/4 miles to Clark Rd. on right.*

Connecticut: Other Places

Archdiocesan Spirit Life Center, 467 Bloomfield Ave., **Bloomfield,** CT 06002. (203) 243-2374

Ingraham House, 156 Summer St., **Bristol,** CT 06010. (203) 582-8422

Our Lady of Calvary Retreat House, 31 Colton St., **Farmington,** CT 06032. (203) 677-8519

Episcopal Camp and Conference Center, Bushy Hill Rd., P.O. Box 577, **Ivoryton,** CT 06442. (203) 767-0848

My Father's House, 39 N. Moodus Rd., Box 22, **Moodus,** CT 06469. (203) 873-1581

Edmundite Apostolate and Conference Center, Enders Island, **Mystic,** CT 06355. (203) 536-0565

Trinita Ecumenical Center, Town Hill Rd., **New Hartford,** CT 06057. (203) 379-8133

Emmaus-Diocesan Spiritual Life Center, 24 Maple Ave., **Uncasville,** CT 06382. (203) 848-3427

Holy Family Retreat House, 303 Tunxis Rd., **West Hartford,** CT 06107. (203) 521-0440

Immaculata Retreat House, Windham Rd., **Willimantic,** CT 06226. (203) 423-8484

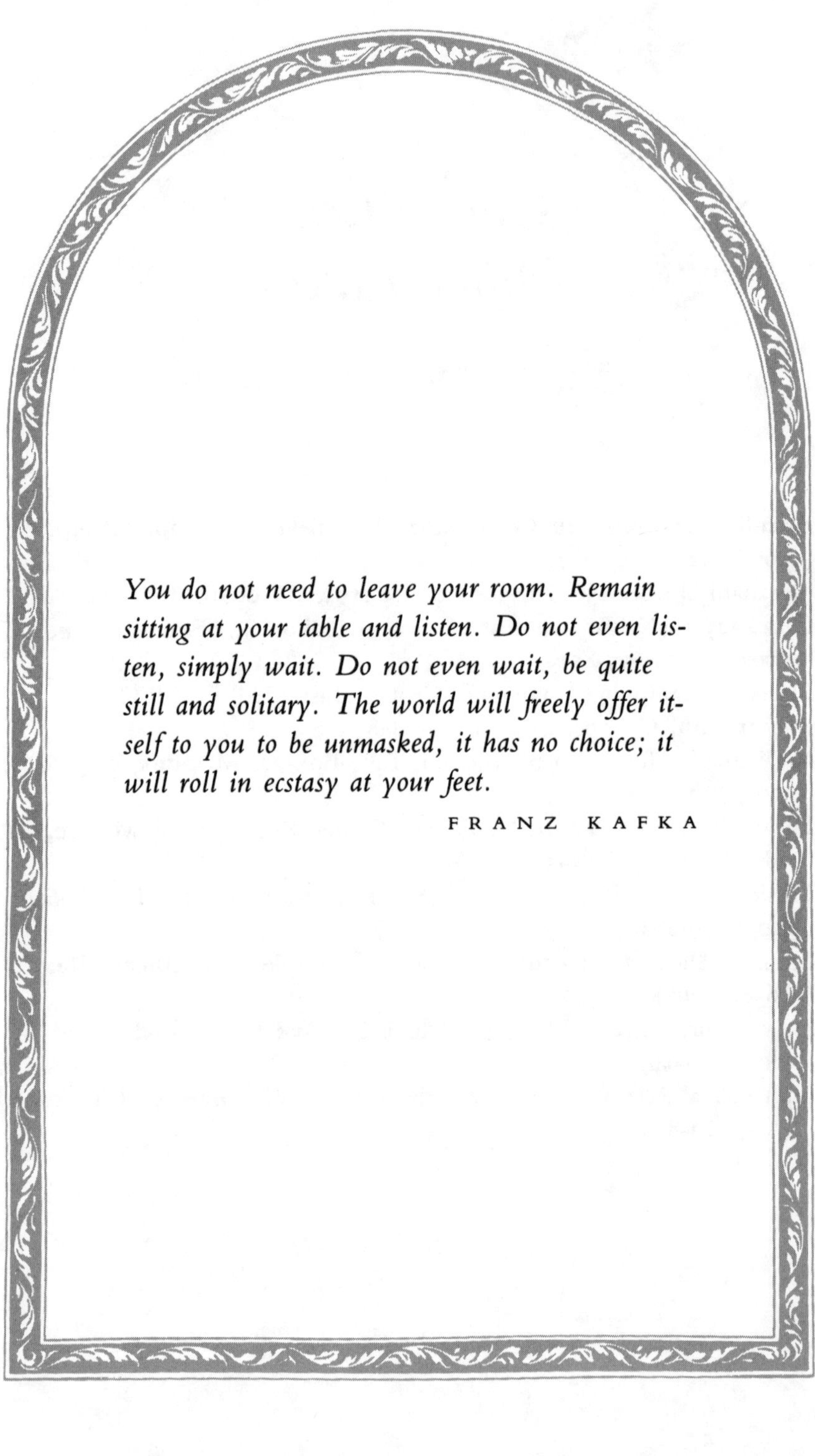

You do not need to leave your room. Remain sitting at your table and listen. Do not even listen, simply wait. Do not even wait, be quite still and solitary. The world will freely offer itself to you to be unmasked, it has no choice; it will roll in ecstasy at your feet.

FRANZ KAFKA

Maine

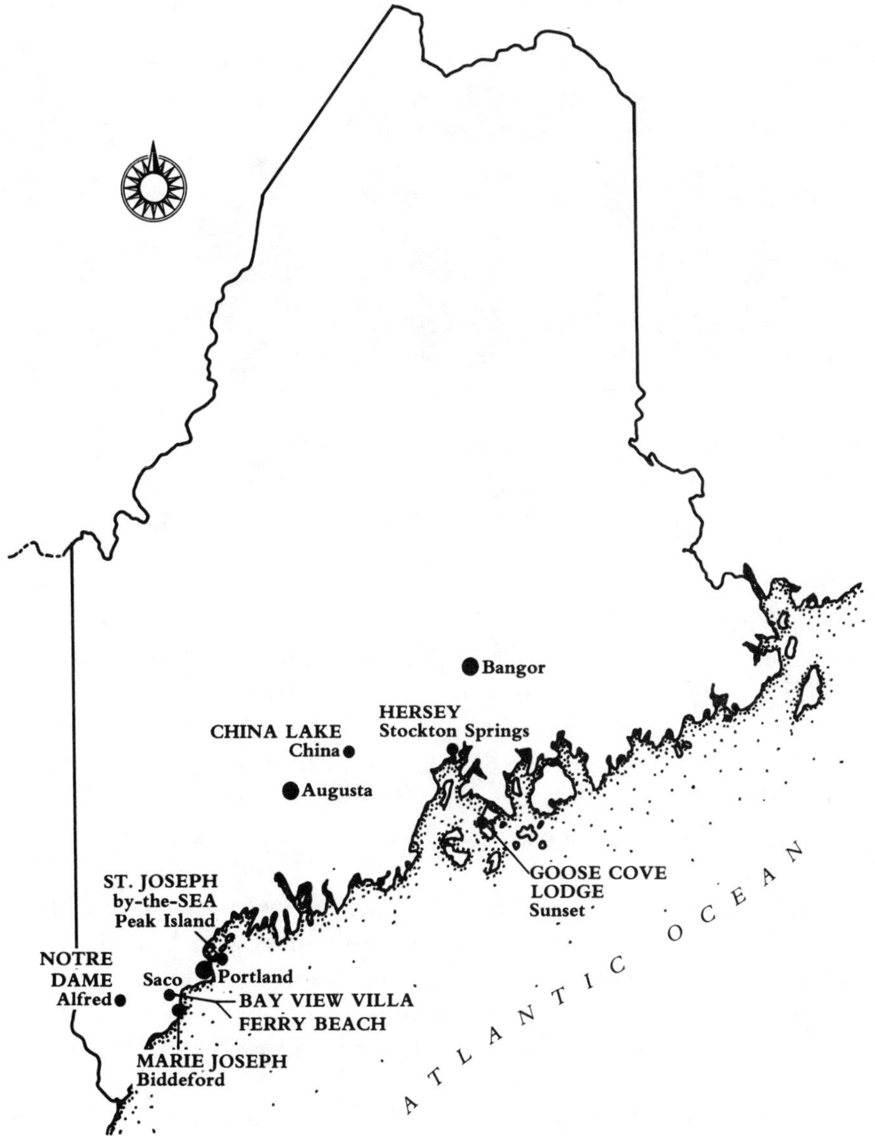
Bangor
HERSEY
Stockton Springs
CHINA LAKE
China
Augusta
GOOSE COVE
LODGE
Sunset
ST. JOSEPH
by-the-SEA
Peak Island
NOTRE
DAME
Alfred
Saco
Portland
BAY VIEW VILLA
FERRY BEACH
MARIE JOSEPH
Biddeford
ATLANTIC OCEAN

Bay View Villa
Saco, ME

Bay View Villa, a lovely, oceanfront retreat center, also serves as a convent home for 32 nuns of the Servants of the Immaculate Heart of Mary. For more than 40 years, the nuns have shared their quiet haven with those seeking a serene, restful atmosphere. There are 28 beds in 18 rooms for individuals or groups for one night, a week, a month, or whatever is needed. The rooms are newly decorated, clean, and bright. Some have a private bath, others share communal washrooms.

The sisters themselves do not organize retreats, but meet daily in the chapel for morning prayer before daily mass, which is said by the resident chaplain about 7:30 A.M. The community meets again for evening prayer around 5:45, before supper. Guests are welcome to join in these daily services. The chapel is one of the main rooms in the hotel and is always open.

The dining room has picture windows looking out onto Saco Bay. There are generous screened porches and spacious grounds; Old Orchard Beach, just a few steps away, offers an uninterrupted seven-mile walk around the bay.

Bay View Villa Guest and Retreat House by the Sea
Rte. 9/187 Bay View Rd.
Saco, ME 04072
(207) 283-3636

Accommodations: *18 newly decorated rooms for men, women, and children over 5 years of age; 3 meals available in dining room overlooking Saco Bay; beachfront, bathhouse, boardwalk; open year-round; seasonal rates $25–$50 singles; $26–$68 doubles (includes breakfast only).*

Directions: *Take U.S. 1 to Rte. 9 East, about 4 miles to Bay View Rd. and the villa.*

China Lake Conference Center

China, ME

Just 30 minutes from Augusta, the China Lake Conference Center, owned by the American Baptist Churches of Maine, is situated on the shores of China Lake. With 200 feet of lakefront and 200 acres of open fields and woods, the center has year-round facilities to accommodate up to 100 people in modern rooms. There are also hilltop cabins available in summer, when children come for camp.

Each year, more than 200 Christian groups use the facilities for purposes as varied as weight loss to a Catholic retreat for teenagers. The center usually caters to groups of ten or more, but can handle private retreats. It is possible for two or more groups to visit at the same time.

The chapel can be used as a place of worship or a meeting hall. The grounds are well kept, with open fields for hikes, and the general atmosphere is fresh, clean, and friendly.

China Lake Conference Center
Rte. *3,* ***Box*** *149*
China, ME *04926*
(207) 968-2101

Accommodations: *Doubles and dormitories for 90 men, women, and children in winter, in 4 houses and a new building; in summer, cabins for* *boys and girls in summer camp (camping grounds expand those numbers); dining room available for 10 or more; 200 acres, 200 feet of shoreline on China Lake; athletic fields, acres of field and forest; open year-round; bunks $7 a night, doubles $10 a night, Williams Cottage on the lake shore, with a capacity of 10 people, is $250 a week; linen $2 a day; 3 family-style meals $12 a day.*

Directions: *Take U.S. 1 toward Belfast, then Rte. 3 West to China Lake, to Rte. 202/9 (Lakeview Dr.); turn right at the BANGOR-CHINA sign, and bear right to the blinking yellow light, then bear left and go 1 1/2 miles past the post office and general store. A sign on the right reads CHINA LAKE CONFERENCE CENTER.*

Ferry Beach Park Association

Saco, ME

The Ferry Beach Park Association, an affiliate of the Unitarian Universalist Church, stands on 30 acres of beachfront and pine woods on Saco Bay. In 1901 the Universalists held a summer meeting here as guests of the owners, the Boston and Maine Railroad, and in 1904 made an initial purchase to acquire a permanent place for their annual meetings. Since then they have purchased more land and have gradually added buildings and programs so that now there is a full season of supervised conference programs. The aim is to encourage a sense of community through self-awareness, personal growth, and responsibility in communal relationships so that everyone is able to make a real contribution to society.

The schedule begins each year in June and continues through early September, the prime weather season for southern Maine. The programs are family-oriented, and some meetings are for children of specific age groups. There are nature courses for exploring the seacoast, and hiking and bicycling trips, plus topics that touch current issues like single parenting and gay rights, as well as fine arts from poetry appreciation to a chamber-music week—just the topics to pursue in a relaxed, healthy, beautiful environment. The programs are Unitarian-oriented, but people of all faiths are welcome.

The accommodations are rough-hewn, summer-camp style, in three buildings. Guests are encouraged to bring sleeping bags or their own linens. There are communal washrooms. Life here is meant to be lived mainly outside, and the generous porches encourage that. The Quillen, a former hotel, is the center of activity, and meals are served in its main dining room.

There is also a camping grove under the supervision of the Wagonmaster, with 35 sites for tents or trailers. Daily services are held at the outdoor chapel by the minister of the week, who is also available for individual counseling. The chapel is a platform surrounded by tall pines that give the place a cathedral-like feeling.

The considerate, competent people who administer Ferry Beach make sure that the reason for its existence is never forgotten. Time here allows one to experience a true sense of fellowship with others and with nature while growing intellectually, emotionally, and spiritually.

Ferry Beach Park Association
5 Morris Ave.
***Saco, ME** 04072*
(207) 282-4489

Accommodations: *Camplike setting for 150 men, women, and children; community dining hall; daily chapel; 30 acres on ocean, tennis courts; open last week of June through August; (Elderhostels early June, and September to mid-October); $15 membership and $20 a night.*

Directions: *Take U.S. 1 to Saco; Rte. 9 East to Bayview Rd. Watch for Ferry Beach Park Association sign (*not *Ferry Beach State Park sign).*

Goose Cove Lodge
Sunset, ME

Some years ago a naturalist bought this promontory of Deer Isle, built a cabin where the main lodge is now, and gave lectures and led nature walks, carving out trails through the pine trees and along the rock ledges at the edge of the sandy beach.

The current owners acquired the 70-acre preserve in the early 1980s and built the main lodge to fit into the raw, natural beauty of the Maine seacoast. The lodge and cabins are tucked away, a few minutes' walk from each other, at one with the unspoiled nature of the island. The cabins have fireplaces and private baths and are comfortably furnished. Many have a private deck where one can sit and look out on the cove. Excellent meals are served in the main lodge. The dining room has a grand vista of the sweep of the cove and the islands beyond in East Penobscot Bay.

There are ten rooms in an annex off the main lodge, as well as the 11 cottages that sleep two to six persons.

Though there is a spot on the property called "Prayer Rock," there is no spiritual affiliation here, apart from the relationship with nature. This is a peaceful outpost at the End of Beyond where hikers, naturalists, bird-watchers, and chair-sitters can find natural beauty and solitude.

Goose Cove Lodge
Deer Isle
***Sunset, ME** 04683*
(207) 348-2508
***Winter:** (207) 767-3003*

Accommodations: *Rooms for 60 men, women, and children in the main lodge, or private cottages with fireplaces and kitchenettes; delicious breakfasts and dinners included in-season, and breakfasts off-season; 70 acres overlooking Penobscot Bay; walking trails along the cliffs beside the sea; excellent book and tape library; open mid-May to mid-October; $520–$800 per person per week includes service and tax during season; $100–$125 a couple per day (with 2-day minimum) during off-season; sliding scale for children; group rates available.*

Directions: *Take U.S. 1 to 4 miles north of Bucksport; turn right onto Rte. 15 (Blue Hill, Deer Isle) to Deer Isle village; turn right on Sunset Rd. and drive 3 miles; watch for sign on right; turn right and follow the road 1 1/2 miles through the woods to the lodge.*

Hersey Retreat

Stockton Springs, ME

In 1875, Samuel Hersey donated this beautiful 25 acres to the First Universalist Church of Bangor. In 1884 the first retreats were held here, making it the oldest Unitarian Universalist conference center. The main building, a handsome lodge, sits on a high point looking out to where the Penobscot River flows into Penobscot Bay. The wraparound porch faces water on three sides, with acres of fields allowing clear views of the islands in the bay.

Meetings are held on the main floor of the lodge, which has a large hall and recreation rooms. The rustic building seems to flow to the outside, with French doors leading to the porch. Upstairs there are nine rooms with 26 beds. Guests should bring their own linens or sleeping bags.

There are two other buildings that can accommodate 18. One of these, the French House, is the oldest building in Waldo County. A restored farmhouse, it serves as the dining facility on the main floor and has 11 beds upstairs. The food here has been much praised, and in 1986 the chef published a cookbook, *What's Cooking at Hersey Retreat,* sharing her secrets about American food.

Conference-retreat programs are held May through October, ranging from writers' workshops to local UU church weekends to youth weeks and family camps to a religious education week with

UU orientation. There are also weeks set aside for Elderhostel, a nonsectarian education program.

This is a secluded, picturesque spot where seals and ospreys share the terrain. Ideal for those who like rustic living and appreciate being close to nature.

Hersey Retreat
***P.O. Box** 1183*
***Stockton Springs, ME** 04981*
(207) 722-3405
***Winter: P.O. Box** 810*
***Brooks, Maine** 04921*
(207) 722-3405

Accommodations: *40 beds—singles, doubles, and bunks—for men, women, and children in the main house; 9 singles in French House, a restored farmhouse; a 4-bedroom guesthouse is available; family-style meals, made by cookbook-author chef, served in French House; beach, meadows, woods, nearby lakes, and normal indoor and outdoor summer-camp activities; open May through October, with planned programs in July and August, including Family Camp, Youth Camp, Elderhostels; adults, $175 a week; ages 5–18, $90 a week; children under 5, $80 a week; the guesthouse can be rented for $300–$400 a week.*

Directions: *Turn off U.S. 1 in Stockton Springs, opposite Rocky Ridge Motel. Cross the railroad tracks; take the first right to the end of the road, about one mile.*

Marie Joseph Spiritual Center
Biddeford, ME

In 1947 the Sisters of the Presentation of Mary acquired the Ocean View Hotel as their provincial house. They operated a boarding school for ten years, then ran a day-care center and held evening education classes until 1976, when they concentrated their efforts into the Spiritual Center. The center is less than 100 yards from a low, sandy shore that offers miles of beach walking.

The huge, sparkling white building is home to 17 nuns, and has additional rooms for 70 retreatants. Guests can join the community in morning prayer at 7:30, daily mass at 8, midday prayers at 11:45, and vespers at 4:30 P.M. Inside the chapel, one feels as though one is at sea; windows on both sides look onto the ocean north and south.

The rooms are comfortable and clean, and there is an elevator to all floors. There are sitting rooms and other places for quiet reading and reflection. Meals are taken in the large dining room, where coffee, tea, and snacks are always available.

The nuns are followers of Blessed Anne Marie Rivier, whose desire to make Jesus Christ known to all inspires and sustains the endeavors of the group. The order offers programs to persons of all faiths, cultures, and life-styles. There are workshops on the monastic way of prayer and on the Enneagram (developed by Sufi masters as a tool for bringing insight into divine activity within the individual), charismatic weekends, directed retreats for those who prefer a daily meeting with a spiritual advisor, and also private retreats.

The building seems to rest peacefully at the edge of the ocean, a short drive from a residential area, but the energy is such that one guest remarked "My goodness—your God here works 24 hours a day!"

Marie Joseph Spiritual Center
***RFD** 2*
***Biddeford, ME** 04005*
(207) 284-5671

Accommodations: *70 men and women are housed in 46 rooms; cafeteria meals; daily mass and morning and evening prayer; directly on beach and ocean; closed first 2 weeks of both June and September; rates vary.*

Directions: *From I-95, take Exit 4 to Rte. 111 East; go straight at the traffic lights past Welby Drugs and Alex Pizza, and take a right on Rte. 9/208 (the Pool Rd.); go 6 miles to Rte. 208 (bear left at water tower) and follow the winding road across a small bridge to a stop sign; turn left onto Beach Rd.; pass the fire station and watch for the sign on the right. The center is in a large building at the end of a long drive.*

Notre Dame Spiritual Center
Alfred, ME

In 1930 the Brothers of Christian Instruction, a Catholic teaching order that also runs Notre Dame University, purchased 400 acres of land and buildings from the Shaker community that had settled here in 1796. The brothers used the property as a seminary until 1956, then as a junior high school until 1980, when they opened a retreat and conference center. They offer a full series of conferences and retreats, and make the facilities available to groups for their own meetings, from teenage confirmation classes to AA retreats. The center is also used by Methodists, Episcopalians, and Congregationalists.

The attraction of this place is the peaceful atmosphere and the well-kept buildings that were designed and built in the Shaker tradition. In 1845, Shaker membership totaled nearly 4,000 in 18 communities from Maine to Kentucky. A list of innovations and improvements made by Shakers reflects ingenuity out of proportion to their numbers. Credited with developing the flat broom, the washing machine, a revolving oven, and an efficient woodburning stove, the Shakers sought efficiency in order to have more time for prayer. Their woodcrafts, carved elegantly and simply, were precise examples of work with a purpose expressed in the Shaker maxim: "Do all your work as though you had a thousand years to live, and as you would if you knew you must die tomorrow."

Today there are only a handful of Shakers, and in the mid-1960s the parent ministry closed the covenant, barring new members. Those few remaining accept the situation, believing their values will endure somehow. One way for them to be remembered is to pass on their buildings to a caring group like the brothers who maintain this center, making the facilities available to spiritually oriented, conscientious, and respectful people.

One of the buildings, a former faculty house, has been renovated by a group who holds regular charismatic prayer meetings every Friday evening. The first floor has been completely restored to its former Shaker glory.

The brothers have a daily mass and late-afternoon prayer service before the evening meal taken in a large cafeteria. The modern chapel is big enough for 100 worshipers. The sleeping rooms are in two buildings, so different groups can be there at the same time, following their own schedule and purpose without any conflict.

The sense of spiritual purpose is still very evident in this place.

Notre Dame Spiritual Center
Alfred, ME 04002
(207) 324-6160 or 324-6612 (Monday–Friday, 9 A.M.–4 P.M.)

Accommodations: *33 very simple bedrooms for 84 men, women, and children; inviting homemade buffet meals; mass and vespers daily; 400 acres, lake, tennis court, 3,000 apple trees; bakery on property; open year-round (Elderhostels mid-June through August); $25 a night.*

Directions: *From I-95, take Exit 4 (Biddeford-Alfred). Turn right on Rte. 111 West. Drive about 12 miles to the traffic light at Junction 202-4; turn right on 202 East; after the Alfred village square, continue for about 1 mile and watch for the sign reading* BROTHERS OF CHRISTIAN INSTRUCTION, NOTRE DAME—SPIRITUAL CENTER. *Drive up the hill to the very top.*

St. Joseph-by-the-Sea
Peaks Island, ME

Just a three-mile ferry ride from Portland is 720-acre Peaks Island, where some independent New Englanders reside year-round, commuting daily to the mainland. This is also home to an energetic, committed group of nuns, the Sisters of Notre Dame. Part of an international congregation founded in 1804 in France, the order has 3,000 nuns with ministries in 14 countries.

In the mid-1960s the sisters acquired Oak Cottage, previously owned by one of the five families who originally settled Peaks. Built in 1864 to house a large family, it eventually became a rooming house for summer visitors. There were nine guest rooms then, but only one bathroom, so each bedroom had a "thunder jug," or one could use the outhouse. The sisters have introduced modern plumbing, and there are now 12 comfortable, clean, single rooms in a wing behind the chapel that is connected to the main house. There are indoor communal washrooms.

There is a mass daily, either at a nearby parish church or in the lovely, paneled chapel where the nuns say morning office and evening vespers, and guests are welcome. The nuns are all Eucharist ministers, which enables them to minister to island shut-ins and retreatants.

There is a multifaceted retreat and vacation orientation, even though the sisters play an integral part in the island community.

Despite the numerous activities, there is a great feeling of calm as the nuns go about their duties, maintaining silence out of respect for each other and those who have come here in search of peace and solitude.

One can wander down the hill to the beach, or follow the road to the eastern shore and walk for hours, feeling the slow pace of island life. Perhaps the best description of St. Joseph's can be borrowed from an historic account of the old car ferry *Swampscott,* which used to serve the island: "She was warm and snug and ran all winter."

St. Joseph-by-the-Sea
203 ***Pleasant Ave.***
Peaks Island, ME *04108*
(207) 766-2284

Accommodations: *12 singles for men and women; family-style meals; morning prayer, mass (sometimes on video), and vespers daily; beach and country lane walking on this 720-acre island; closed December and January; $25 a night laity; $15 religious. When writing for reservations, give reason for coming.*

Directions: *Casco Bay Line ferry from Portland, Maine. From I-95, take Exit 6A to I-295 North to the Franklin St. exit, which leads to the Casco Bay Lines and the waterfront. Leave your car in the garage, and you will be picked up at the ferry; or call ahead for directions if you are taking your car to the island.*

Maine: Other Places

St. Paul's Retreat House and Cursillo Center, 136 State St., **Augusta,** ME 04330. (207) 622-6235

Kanzeon Zen Center, 33 Ledgelawn Ave., **Bar Harbor,** ME 04609. (207) 288-3569

St. Benedict's House, P.O. Box 4383, RR 1, **Camden,** ME 04843. (207) 763-4020

Rockcraft Lodge, **East Sebago,** ME 04029. (207) 787-2876

Oceanwood, **Ocean Park,** ME 04063. (207) 934-9655

Northern Pines, Rte. 85, RR 1, P.O. Box 279, **Raymond,** ME 04071. (207) 655-7624

Morgan Bay Zendo, Morgan Bay Rd., **Surry,** ME 04684. (207) 667-5428

Servants of the Cross, Skyhigh Prayer Summit, 85A Meadow Rd., **Topsham,** ME 04086. (207) 725-7577

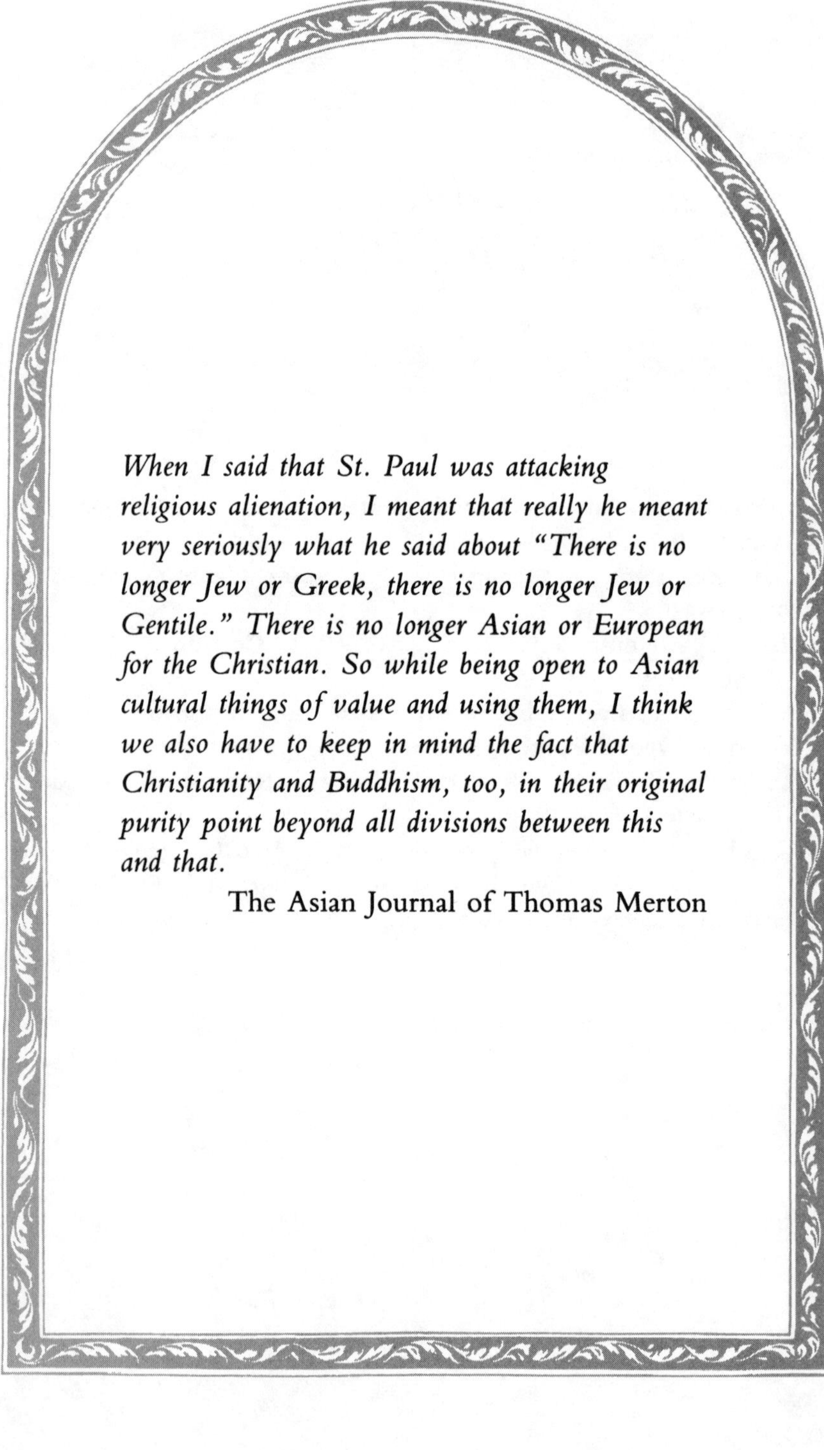

When I said that St. Paul was attacking religious alienation, I meant that really he meant very seriously what he said about "There is no longer Jew or Greek, there is no longer Jew or Gentile." There is no longer Asian or European for the Christian. So while being open to Asian cultural things of value and using them, I think we also have to keep in mind the fact that Christianity and Buddhism, too, in their original purity point beyond all divisions between this and that.

The Asian Journal of Thomas Merton

Massachusetts

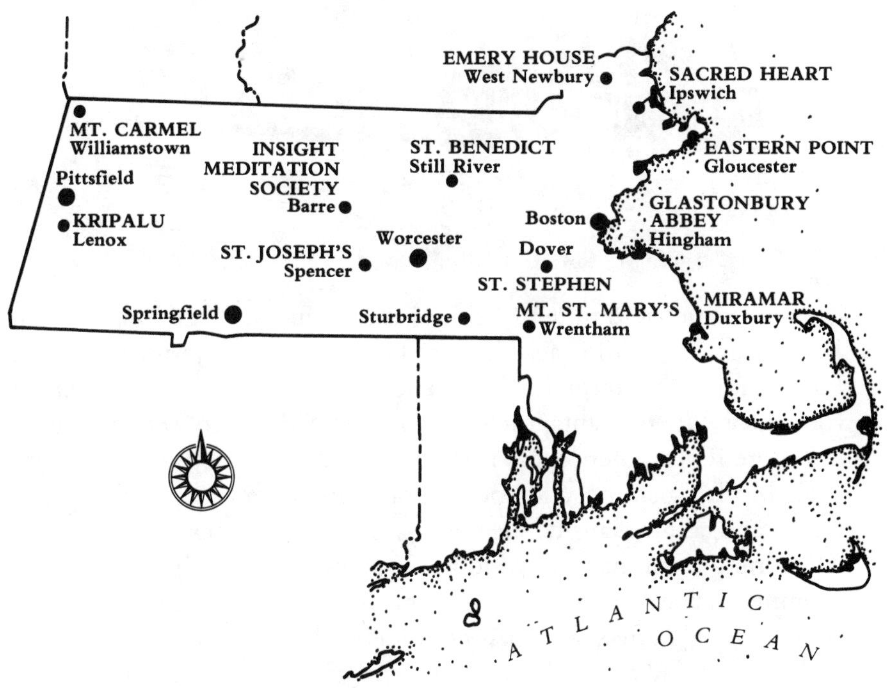

Eastern Point Retreat House

Gloucester, MA

This magnificent granite mansion was built in 1921, and looks out on Brace's Cove and the back shore of Gloucester. The Jesuit Fathers of New England acquired it in 1957 and added a wing to provide single rooms for 50 retreatants, each with a dramatic view of the sea. There is a large foyer where mass is said daily, and a variety of rooms are available for reading and meditation. Guests appreciate the many nooks and crannies inside the house and along the rocks by the shore. The dining room has bay windows looking out over the ocean. Each evening, taped classical music is played to accompany the buffet supper. Tea, coffee, and snacks are available all day.

There is a full schedule of guided and directed retreats throughout the year, given by the staff of six Jesuits. The length of the retreats varies from a weekend to a full month, and there is a special week for Jesuits only. Some weekends are reserved for AA meetings.

The aim of the programs is to help people discover where they are now and enable them to proceed to the next stage in their development, using scriptural study, drawing, and body movement. The 30-day retreats are conducted primarily in silence, with two "break" days. The atmosphere of silence and the closeness to the sea facilitate the process. "The longest journey," one staff member said, "is from the head to the gut."

People may come with problems or unresolved decisions, but here they have a chance to leave all this baggage at the gate and concentrate on strengthening and deepening their relationship with the Lord.

Eastern Point Retreat House
Gonzaga
Gloucester, MA *01930*
(508) 283-0013

Accommodations: *Private rooms for 48–52 men and women in this great mansion and attached wing; plain, buffet-style meals, in silence, in a dining room overlooking the sea; daily mass; country lanes for walking; open year-round; $50 a night.*

Directions: *About an hour north of Boston, Eastern Point can be reached via Rte. 128 North to the very end, proceeding through the 2 traffic circles and 2 sets of traffic lights. At the last light, proceed straight through and up a hill to the left. Follow East Main St. past Niles Beach on your right, and between 2 stone pillars marked* PRIVATE: EASTERN POINT. *Follow this little road through twists and turns until you see signs to the retreat house.*

Emery House
West Newbury, MA

In 1635, the Emery family arrived by ship from England; they acquired this property in 1680. It remained in the family until 1954, when the last Emery died and bequeathed it to the Anglican Society of St. John the Evangelist. This beautifully rustic 120 acres is at the confluence of the Merrimack and Artichoke rivers, down a quiet road on the outskirts of West Newbury.

The main house dates from 1745. It has been carefully refurbished and retains its original quality and charm. A later addition is the stunning chapel with windows that look over the fields to the rivers beyond. The monks meet here to pray four times a day. After the last service, Compline, at 9 P.M., silence is observed until 9 A.M. the next day.

There are five lovely, modern hermitages nestled together some distance below the main house. Each is self-sufficient, with a kitchenette where basics are provided for pickup breakfast, as well as a private bath, woodburning stove, and comfortable bed and furnishings. The hermitages are just a few minutes' walk from the main house, where meals are served; lunch is provided after Eucharist, and dinner after the evening prayer. The food is delicious.

The monks are a community of priests and brothers who take lifetime vows of poverty, celibacy, and obedience. The order was founded in England in 1866 by Father Richard Meux Benson, the vicar of Cowley; thus they are often referred to as the Cowley Monks, and are the oldest Anglican religious order for men. Their main monastery in the United States is St. Mary and St. John, located in Cambridge, Massachusetts.

Emery House is not only a retreat sanctuary for the Cowley Monks; it also offers regular weekend programs to laypeople and couples of any faith who seek to deepen their spiritual lives. Private retreatants are welcome. The beautifully maintained house and hermitages, the considerate and friendly staff, and the peaceful quality of the place serve its purpose well.

Emery House
The Society of St. John the Evangelist
Emery Lane
***West Newbury, MA** 01985*
(508) 462-7940

Accommodations: *Rooms for 11 men and women or 8 couples in the 18th-century main house and 5 beautiful hermitages with kitchenettes; delicious meals served with the community in the main house; prayer 4 times daily; birding, boating on rivers, fishing, hiking on extensive property; closed 6 P.M. Sunday to 5:30 P.M. Monday, as well as first 2 weeks of June and month of August; suggested donation: $30–$40 a night.*

Directions: *Emery House is about an hour's drive from downtown Boston. Take I-95 North to Exit 57 (Rte. 113—Newburyport/West Newbury). Drive west on Rte. 113 toward West Newbury for 1 mile. The turn for Emery House is marked by a gray sign on the right side of the road as you go up a small hill.*

Glastonbury Abbey
Hingham, MA

The Benedictine monks first came to this quiet neighborhood in 1954, when they acquired an old estate with 25 acres of woodlands bordered by stone fences. They currently own about 60 acres of very appealing landscape. The abbey buildings are dominated by a stone tower, which the original owners built for ornamental purposes and used as a giant gazebo for entertaining. All of the original buildings have been adapted for monastery use: the administration building was formerly a barn and stable; Whiting House, now one of the guesthouses, was the home of the groundskeeper; and Stonecrest, the other guesthouse, was that of a Methodist missionary.

The modern chapel, tucked away behind the monastery, is the only new building. The architect was a friend of the monks and looked on the project as a labor of love. He designed the freestanding altar, the triangular windows, the benches, and even the candlesticks. Much of the artwork is brightly colored acrylic or plaster on wood, and there are dignified, though cartoonlike, Stations of the Cross. Here the monks sing the canonical hours five times a day from 6:30 A.M. to 7:45 P.M. Mass is said at noon, except on Sunday, when it is at 9:30 A.M. About ten monks sing the liturgy in deep, rich tones, and guests are invited to join in the singing. Much of the

organ music that accompanies the singing was composed by one of the resident brothers. Known as Black Benedictines because of their black, cowled habits, the monks say the office in the vernacular and devote at least three hours a day to prayer. During the course of a week, 75 psalms will be chanted. The chapel is open from 6:30 A.M. to 9 P.M.

Private retreatants are welcome for one night, but a few days' stay is preferable. Monks are available on request for individual guidance or the Sacrament of Reconciliation. People are also encouraged to come for a weekend of spiritual restoration. These weekends begin Friday at 7 P.M. and conclude Sunday afternoon. All retreatants are requested to observe silence in the retreat houses.

Glastonbury Abbey
The Retreat House
16 Hull St.
***Hingham, MA** 02043*
(617) 749-2155

Accommodations: *30 private rooms for men and women, in 2 comfortable guesthouses; pickup breakfasts; lunch and dinner with monks, or delivered to a guesthouse if more than 6 are dining; canonical hours with lovely singing; 60 wooded acres with some marked trails; weeding volunteers needed; open year-round, except for personal retreats of monks (closed Sunday nights, September to May); suggested donation: $35 a night.*

Directions: *From Boston, take I-93 South (Southeast Expressway) to Rte. 3 South (toward Cape Cod) to Exit 14, (Rte. 228, Rockland/Hingham); follow Rte. 228 North (Main St., Hingham) about 7 miles to the abbey.*

Insight Meditation Society
Barre, MA

In 1975 a group of Americans who had studied Vipassana (insight meditation) in Southeast Asia realized that it would be beneficial to have a center in the United States, used exclusively for Vipassana retreats. In 1976 they acquired a Georgian brick mansion built by a prominent Boston family in the early 1900s. Located on 80 acres of secluded land in northwest Massachusetts, near Worcester, the mansion was used as a rest home in the 1940s, and as a novitiate for Blessed Sacrament priests and brothers in the 1950s and 1960s.

The Buddha said, "We are shaped by our thoughts; we become what we think. When the mind is pure, joy follows, like a shadow that never leaves." Vipassana meditation aims to free the mind of greed, hatred, and delusion. The meditation practice at IMS is an investigation of the mind-body process through focused awareness. The student learns to observe from a place of stillness, seeing life as a constantly changing process, and seeking to accept whatever takes place with equanimity and balance.

Retreats can be as short as two days or as long as 12 weeks. Silence is observed at all times. There is a nightly discourse given by the retreat director, and individuals have an interview every other day. The double rooms are spartan, with foam pads for sleeping. Bring your own linens or sleeping bag. There are separate floors for men and women, with community washrooms.

A typical day begins at 5 A.M. and ends at 10 P.M. There are alternating periods of sitting (four per day) and walking meditation. There is also a 45-minute work period devoted to tasks such as cleaning or helping with meal preparation. (All food served is vegetarian.) Students are asked to refrain from reading, writing, phone calls, and any other distractions from meditation practice.

It is an extraordinary experience to join a group of people who do not talk, listen to the radio, watch television, or escape into some other activity, but are simply content to meditate. As one expressed it, "A great feeling of bliss comes over you, and a oneness with others, a pure feeling of love." Not surprisingly, IMS is generally fully booked, and asks those interested to plan far ahead.

Insight Meditation Society
Pleasant St.
Barre, MA *01005*
(508) 355-4378

Accommodations: *For men and women, 100 singles and doubles (a family course is given in summer); buffet-style vegetarian meals are served in the large dining room; sitting and walking meditation daily; courses run from 2 days on a weekend to 3 months; silence is maintained except for teacher interviews and evening discourse; 45-minute work period daily; open year-round; $18.50 min. a night; $45 for 2-day weekend retreat; resident work/study programs are available.*

Directions: *From Worcester, MA, take Rte. 122A North 23 miles to Barre; Insight Meditation Society is 3 miles north of Barre on Rte. 122A.*

Kripalu Center for Yoga and Health
Lenox, MA

In the early 1980s the followers of Yogi Amrit Desai acquired this huge building located next to the Tanglewood Music Festival grounds. It was built in the 1950s by the Jesuits as a seminary with a capacity for 600, but very few novices materialized, and the property was left vacant for ten years until Kripalu took it over. It is so large that four acres of carpet were purchased to cover the floors.

Named after Yogi Amrit Desai's teacher, Swami Kripalvananda, the center offers a wide range of programs focusing on holistic health education, yoga, and meditation. There are rest and renewal programs for those who need time to catch up with themselves, a great variety of workshops, and a three-month Spiritual Lifestyle Training Program.

There is a wide choice of accommodations from dormitory to private single or double rooms with bath. Vegetarian food is provided in the large dining hall. Meals are generally eaten in silence. There is a staff and student body of 300, and rooms for 270 guests, which are usually filled Yet, despite the number of people coming and going, there is a lively spirit of helpfulness and consideration, and the flow of people is quiet and purposeful.

The former chapel has been turned into a large meditation hall by taking out the pews and carpeting the floor. The mosaic on the back wall of Saint Ignatius Loyola, the founder of the Society of Jesus, provides an interesting backdrop to the platform in front of it that holds large photos of Swami Kripalvananda and Yogi Desai. "Three saints," one observer remarked. "Yes," said a staff member, "but I'm not so sure of the one on the wall."

Traditional religion has a dogma and creed suggesting that believers will be saved. In yogic practice, the spiritual and the practical go hand in hand; one lives the practice by sharing it: Show a better way; do not *talk* a better way. Through diet, exercise, and meditation, Kripalu attempts to quicken the spiritual energy of those who are ready. This is an invitation to discover through personal experience and experimentation what the rules of life really are. The supportive atmosphere of love and acceptance allows guests and students to observe themselves honestly, to start to cleanse their lives through attention to detail, and to handle reality in a compassionate way. The staff is available for counseling, but considerate of the need for solitude.

There is also a holistic doctor and a large team of massage and other bodywork therapists; appointments with these are very popular, so bookings should be made at the time of reservation.

The center looks over a lake, a short walk downhill, which has a public beach. There are many hiking trails through the pines and the Tanglewood grounds nearby.

Kripalu Center for Yoga and Health
***P.O. Box** 793*
***Lenox, MA** 02140*
(413) 637-3280

Accommodations: *Rooms for 270 men, women, and supervised children in singles, doubles, and dorms; vegetarian meals, usually taken in silence; daily meditation, yoga, a variety of courses for rest and renewal; lake, hiking trails; childcare sometimes available; open year-round; $50–$115 a night.*

Directions: *From I-90, take Exit B-3 (Rte. 22, Austerlitz/New Lebanon). Follow Rte. 22 South for 7/10 mile and turn left onto Rte. 102 East. Stay on Rte. 102 for 2 1/2 miles into West Stockbridge. Continue another 3 1/2 miles to the junction of Rtes. 102 and 183; turn left onto 183. The entrance to Kripalu Center is 3.8 miles north of this intersection, on the left, 1/2 mile past the Berkshire Country Day School and just before the intersection of 183 and Richmond Mountain Rd.*

Miramar Retreat Center
Duxbury, MA

When the Roman Catholic Divine Word Missionaries opened a seminary here in 1922 in what was once the summer residence of Boston's Cardinal O'Connell, the Ku Klux Klan burned a cross in the front yard to welcome them. Today the order numbers over 5,000 and teaches in 51 countries. Artifacts from many of these countries decorate the main building.

In 1945 an additional 37 acres were purchased from the Belknap estate, and in 1982 the original seminary buildings were sold and the money used to expand and renovate the retreat center, built on the new land. The center, with its picturesque water tower, has a view of Duxbury and Cape Cod bays, and is only five miles from Plymouth, where the *Mayflower* landed.

There are 30 modern double rooms, each with a private bath. The entire complex is wheelchair-accessible, and many groups who work with the disabled take advantage of this. The dining room, which can seat up to 100, has large windows that look out over the water.

The highly qualified staff of six priests and one brother conduct a regular program of evening and weekend retreats for people of all ages, with themes as varied as coping with stress and anger, and helping children of dysfunctional families. Private retreatants are welcome, and staff members are available for spiritual counseling.

The wood-paneled chapel is the focal point of the complex, and the day begins with morning prayer at 7:10, followed by mass at 7:30. The aim is to provide a peaceful setting where retreatants will open themselves to the spirit and let the Lord work within them. Just being in this place helps one to appreciate the last stanza of Cardinal O'Connell's poem, "Miramar":

For in thy silence, Miramar,
The voice of Heaven I hear;
And in thy calm and sweet repose
I know that God is near.

Miramar Retreat Center
P.O. Box M
***Duxbury, MA** 02332*
(617) 585-2460

Accommodations: *30 doubles with private bath, for men and women; 3 meals daily in the cafeteria; daily mass in a lovely chapel; prayer room; 32 acres overlooking the ocean; 7 miles of beach, 5 minutes away; completely wheelchair-accessible; open year-round; $30 a night.*

Directions: *Miramar is on Duxbury Bay, 35 miles south of Boston, 5 miles north of Plymouth. From Rte. 3, take Exit 10 (Kingston/South Duxbury). Turn north onto Rte. 3A. Drive 1/2 mile to Texaco/Michelin station and turn right. Drive 1/2 mile to Miramar.*

Mount Carmel Retreat House
Williamstown, MA

This 720-acre estate was acquired by the Catholic Carmelite order in the early 1950s from the family of Sinclair Lewis, the first American to win the Nobel Prize for Literature. The original mansion was built in 1916 and named Thorvale, after Thunder Valley, which it faces, and is so called because of the magnificent resounding thunder that can be heard in the valley during a storm. There is an excellent view of Mount Graylock, the highest point in Massachusetts.

Mount Carmel was first used as a novitiate to train priests and brothers in the Carmelite tradition of "contemplatives in action." They trace their heritage back to hermits who lived in caves on the slopes of Mount Carmel in Palestine, devoting their lives to service and inspired by the prophet Elijah, whom they looked on as their spiritual father. In the 12th and 13th centuries, war forced the Carmelites to move. The Catholic Church asked them to bring their love of prayer and solitude to Europe, into cities and rural areas, wherever they were needed. They came to the Americas with the early settlers.

The priests and brothers who live here organize and manage a full range of retreats for families, couples, and individuals, as well as an annual ten-day retreat for clergy, religious, and laity. There are summer meetings focusing on the Enneagram program, and one that draws on the richness of music and art.

The magnificent mansion has 30 rooms for guests, with 60 beds. Each room has a sink, and there are community baths for men and women. There is a large main chapel, a dining room, conference and sitting rooms, and a full gymnasium. There is also a meditation chapel where services are held if only a small number of guests are in residence. The community observes daily mass preceded by morning office and meditation at 7:30 A.M., and meets again at 5 P.M. for vespers. Retreatants are welcome at these services.

There is a separate cottage with five bedrooms, a former caretaker's residence, and a two-bedroom efficiency apartment, a former chicken house constructed by Sinclair Lewis, who was reportedly very proud of it as a state-of-the-art chicken facility in the late 1940s.

Whatever the length of the stay or the focus of a particular program, the days are structured to allow the rhythm and space necessary for each person to attend to the working of the spirit within.

Mount Carmel Retreat House
***Oblong Rd., Box** 613*
***Williamstown, MA** 01267*
(413) 458-3164

Accommodations: *30 private rooms with sinks in the main house for men, women, and children, plus a 5-bedroom cottage and a 2-bedroom cottage with kitchens; daily mass and vespers; rustic chapel in woods; 720 acres; walking trails, stream, Japanese garden, gazebo, swimming pool, tennis court; open year-round; approximately $35 a night, depending on program and accommodations.*

Directions: *From I-90, take Exit 2 (Lee/Pittsfield). At the end of the exit, turn right onto Rte. 20 West and follow through Lee and Lenox toward Pittsfield. Rte. 20 will lead into Rte. 7 North; follow Rte. 7 into southern Williamstown. Pass the intersection of Rtes. 7 and 43 and take first left after Sweetbrook Nursing Home (sign reads CARMELITE FRIARS.) Go along Woodcock Rd. to next sign and turn right onto Oblong Rd. Mt. Carmel will appear on your left after 3/10 mile.*

Mount St. Mary's Abbey
Wrentham, MA

Forty miles west of Boston, a group of 50 Trappistine nuns live in a cloistered community, following the Rule of Saint Benedict. With traditions similar to Trappist monks, they devote their lives to work and prayer. The monastery dates back to the 1940s, when Cardinal Cushing wanted to have Trappistine nuns in the Boston diocese, and helped them find the property. The original 300 acres were bought from businessman John McMahon, who was later to cancel the mortgage and leave an adjoining 300 acres and his substantial summer house to the nuns.

The main monastery building was completed in 1949, and the community, started by three nuns from Ireland, has flourished and sent groups to create other foundations in the United States. Initially, the main source of income came from dairy cows, but in 1956 the nuns began to make Trappistine Quality Candy, which has proved very popular. The Butter Nut-Munch, a hard toffee hand-dipped in milk chocolate and rolled in ground nuts, is a confection inspired by heaven. The monastery still keeps 50 dairy cows—"one for each of us" a nun explained with a smile.

About ten guests can stay on the second floor of the monastery, above the gift shop where convent-made candy, religious articles, and greeting cards are always available. Fresh bread is sold twice a week, and the sweet smell of the loaves is in the air on baking days.

Guest rooms are taken care of by the nuns, who have access through a maze of doors that would baffle and perplex even the most astute burglar.

The McMahon house, across the road from the monastery, has been refurbished recently, and the rooms there are clean and comfortable. Meals are provided, or guests help themselves from the stocked kitchens in both guest areas.

The nuns meet to pray together eight times a day, from 3 A.M. to 7 P.M. The sound of those 50 voices raised in song is unforgettable. Guests are welcome to attend the services, but may not join in the rigorous work of the community. There is a sense of great happiness and contentment in this abbey. As one nun said, "When I entered, I thought I was giving up my liberty, but I've found more real freedom here than I have ever known."

Mount St. Mary's Abbey
300 ***Arnold Rd.***
Wrentham, MA *02093*
(508) 528-1282

Accommodations: *For men, women, and children, 6 rooms with 8 beds, including a 2-bedroom apartment, in the monastery, with a fully stocked kitchen, including homemade bread, fresh eggs, and milk from the abbey farm; McMahon House, a mansion on the property, can accommodate 15 in nine singles and doubles; canonical hours; homemade candy for sale; open year-round; free-will donation.*

Directions: *The abbey is located halfway between Boston and Worcester. At Worcester, take I-495 South to Exit 16 (Franklin/King St.), second exit. Turn right off the exit ramp and make an immediate left turn onto Union St. onto Arnold St. The abbey sign is on your left in about 2 miles. If you reach the Big Apple fruit stand, you've just missed the turn.*

Sacred Heart Retreat House
Ipswich, MA

The main building of this retreat house is a huge brick mansion resembling an English manor. The entrance leads into a large, wood-paneled living room with a fireplace fit for a king. A wide staircase ascends to two balconies leading to a warren of comfortable bedrooms, sharing baths with adjoining rooms.

Off the main room, which is the focal point of the house, are various doorways. One leads to the library, packed with books from floor to ceiling, and containing a long table and chairs for browsing and study. Students attending nearby Gordon Conwell Seminary, a Protestant college, have adopted this Catholic retreat house and often come in the evening to use the library for homework and relaxation.

The large chapel in pale wood seats close to 100; mass is said here at 7 A.M. and evening prayers at 5 P.M. A doorway leads to the dark wood dining room, where delicious meals are served. The young gourmet chef bakes bread for the main meals.

The property is owned by the Catholic Salesians of Saint John Bosco—the patron saint of youth—and is managed by one priest and two brothers, who make the facilities available for group meetings and private retreats. There is another building, primarily used for youth groups, that can house 48.

Each September the local Lions Club holds its "Oktoberfest" here, and more than 15,000 people fill the grounds. On the almost 80 acres of lawns and fields are two baseball diamonds, a soccer field, and outdoor basketball and handball courts. There are also two tennis courts and an outdoor swimming pool.

The popularity of Sacred Heart is evident in the number of organizations that return regularly, and kids who have spent weekends describe the place as "neat," "far out," and "cool."

Sacred Heart Retreat House
Route 1A, Box 567
Ipswich, MA 01938
(508) 356-3838

Accommodations: *Room for 45 men, women, and children in 29 bedrooms, as well as a youth retreat house for 48 in an old stable on this 75-acre estate; delicious meals; daily mass and evening prayer; library, swimming pool, handball, soccer and baseball fields, 2 tennis courts; open year-round; $60 a weekend.*

Directions: *The Sacred Heart Retreat House is 28 miles north of Boston on Rte. 1A, a bit more than a mile south of the center of Ipswich. From I-95, take Rte. 133 East to Rte. 1A. Drive south on Rte. 1A through Ipswich to the Retreat House.*

St. Benedict Priory
Still River, MA

The way to St. Benedict Priory leads through the classic New England small town of Still River. The main street is bordered by one fine house after another, generous wood-frame homes with gingerbread trim and large porches behind well-tended yards. The houses all look as if painters had finished and put away their ladders just in time for the family reunion.

The priory, outside the town, is a 68-acre farm being worked by a professional farmer. The monastery complex is approached by a semicircular drive that leads to the main residence of the monks, the chapel, and the guesthouse; farther along is a parking area and a separate building used for meetings and concerts. Built on a knoll, the monastery buildings look across a wide valley to low mountains; the highest peak is 2,000-foot Mount Wachusetts, some 40 miles away. The grounds around the buildings are carefully maintained, each monk responsible for a section. A rock garden surrounds a back terrace that sits snugly between the monks' residence and the chapel.

Some of the priests say mass and hear confession in neighboring parishes. The monks at home gather to sing the canonical hours in the simple chapel, whose low, beamed ceiling and polished woodwork give a sense of cleanliness and strength.

The two-story guesthouse has small, comfortable rooms with twin beds in each. The rooms have been decorated with care, using mainly donated furniture. There are two or more bathrooms on each floor. Meals are taken family-style, from a sideboard in the dining room. One of the monks is assigned to eat with the guests at evening meal, and, except on Saturday, the entire monastic community comes to talk with the guests after the evening meal.

St. Scholastica Priory is a sister monastery, 45 minutes away in Petersham, Massachusetts. It runs a bakery featuring brownies and Irish soda bread that are also available by mail order. There are guest facilities for ten men with the seven resident monks, and for 12 women with the 21 resident nuns. The priory is well known for its St. Bede's Publications, which specialize in translating European theological writings.

St. Benedict Priory
252 Still River Rd., Box 67
Still River, MA 01467
(508) 456-3221
(508) 724-3213 (St. Scholastica)

Accommodations: *A 35-bedroom guesthouse with singles and doubles for men, women, and children; buffet-style meals, with milk from the priory cows; canonical hours are sung in a lovely chapel; 68 acres and gardens; open year-round; $25 a night. For St. Scholastica Priory, see "Other Places" at the end of the Massachusetts section.*

Directions: *From I-90, take Exit 11A to I-495 North (5 mins.) to Rte. 117 West (5 mins.) to Rte. 110 North (Still River Rd.) to the town of Harvard. Still River is part of Harvard, and the priory is at the southern end of the town on the west side of the road.*

St. Joseph's Abbey
Spencer, MA

In the early 1950s, Brother Blaise Drayton, a Trappist monk, modeled St. Joseph's after the Cistercian abbey of Fontenay in southern France. The monks took much of the stone for the construction from the surrounding fields. The buildings have a medieval look and atmosphere, and house more than 70 monks, some of them retired. The dimly lighted chapel is filled with their deep, rich voices at the canonical hours.

The property consists of 1,800 acres, 1,000 of which are wooded and the rest farmland, some of which is rented to neighboring farmers for alfalfa and field corn. The main income is derived from the famous Trappist Preserves (jams and jellies) that are made here by 15 of the monks and distributed nationwide. Another important income source is the Holy Rood Guild, which makes liturgical vestments.

There are guest facilities for men only, in a separate wing across from the chapel. These are single rooms with private bath, furnished with bed, desk, chair, and reading lamp. Meals are taken in the guests' dining room, and coffee, tea, and snacks are available all day. Retreatants schedule their own time, are welcome at all chapel services, and may talk with the guestmaster each day about monastic life or for spiritual counseling.

There are two regular guest programs for men: on weekends from

Friday afternoon to Sunday following lunch; and in mid-week from Monday afternoon to Friday morning. Guests are not in direct contact with the monastic community, but the guest facilities and schedule follow the contemplative way of life.

This is a formal monastic community, popular with anyone seeking a close look at the Trappist life-style or a place of silence and prayer.

St. Joseph's Abbey
***Spencer, MA** 01562*
(508) 885-3010

Accommodations: *Men only, in 11 private guest rooms; oak dining room for retreatants; two weekly retreats for which reservations must be made far in advance; prayer, rest, reading in conformity with the Trappist way of life; daily conference available; canonical hours; 1,800 acres; open year-round; free-will offering (average donation has been $30–$50 a night).*

Also in Spencer, for women and couples, is Mary House. See "Other Places" at the end of the Massachusetts section, for the address.

Directions: *From I-90 (Massachusetts Turnpike), take the Sturbridge exit to Rte. 20 East. Follow Rte. 20 East 1 mile to Rte. 49 to Spencer. Turn right at the* T *(Rte. 9) and take the very first left turn (1/4 mile) onto Meadow St., then turn left on Rte. 31. On the left, after 3 miles, is a small sign for the abbey.*

St. Stephen Priory Spiritual Life Center
Dover, MA

The main building of St. Stephen Priory is the former mansion of the Cheney family, who built it in the early 1900s. The 76-acre property, just twenty minutes from Boston, borders the Charles River and has paths and trails through the woods and along the river for quiet walks.

The property was acquired in 1949 by the Dominicans, who initially used it as a novitiate house, and since 1971 the priory has offered retreats. There are accommodations for 80 persons, mostly single rooms with community bath. Meals are taken buffet-style in the large dining room.

There is a beautiful chapel in the main house, where mass is celebrated daily. The community gathers for morning and evening prayers, and retreatants are welcome to attend.

The staff consists of four Dominican priests of the Order of Preachers, and three Sisters of Notre Dame. Working together, they offer a full year's schedule of one-day, weekend, and month-long retreats, and also ongoing lecture series to help individuals live a more Christian life. They have an excellent reputation for their

Renewal Program, designed for those who are seeking personal or mission renewal. This is open to both religious and laypeople.

Two staff members, Barbara Metz, SND, and John Burchill, OP, are coauthors of the book *The Enneagram and Prayer,* and are the main presenters of the center's Enneagram workshops. The Enneagram is an ancient, nine-pointed diagram that helps individuals understand the significance of their lives and their relationships to others.

St. Stephen Priory Spiritual Life Center
20 Glen St., Box 370
Dover, MA 02030
(508) 785-0124 (Mon.–Fri., 9:30 A.M.–4:30 P.M.)

Accommodations: *For men and women, 70 singles and 5 doubles; buffet-style meals in a cozy dining room; morning and evening prayer, and mass daily; 76 acres with trails through woods; borders the Charles River; canoeing, swimming pool, tennis, basketball, handball, baseball field, bikes, cross-country skiing; open year-round; $27 a night for laypeople, $22 a night for religious.*

Directions: *I-95 to Rte. 128 south to Rte. 16, through Wellesley into South Natick village. Turn left on Pleasant St., go over the bridge, and take the first right onto Glen St. After 2 miles, the priory is on the right.*

Massachusetts: Other Places

La Salette Center for Christian Living, 947 Park St., **Attleboro,** MA 02703. (508) 222-5410

St. Margaret's Convent, 17 Louisburg Square, **Boston,** MA 02108. (617) 523-1008

Barlin Acres, 284 East Temple St., **Boylston,** MA 01505. (508) 869-6556

La Salette Retreat Center, P.O. Box E, **Brewster,** MA 02631. (508) 747-0330

Cenacle Retreat House, 200 Lake St., **Brighton,** MA 02135. (617) 254-3150

Adelynrood, 46 Elm St., **Byfield,** MA 01922. (508) 462-6721

Society of St. John the Evangelist, Monastery of SS. Mary and John, 980 Memorial Dr., **Cambridge,** MA 02138. (617) 876-3037

Pioneer Valley Zendo, 263 Warnerhill Rd., **Charlemont,** MA 01339. (413) 339-4000

Bement Camp and Conference Center, Drawer F, **Charlton Depot,** MA 01509. (508) 248-7811

Sisters of St. Joseph Retreat Center, 339 Jerusalem Rd., **Cohasset,** MA 02025. (617) 383-6029

Craigville Conference Center, **Craigville,** MA 02636. (617) 775-1265

The Marist House, 518 Pleasant St., **Framingham,** MA 01701. (508) 879-1620

United Church of Christ Conference Center, Salem End and Badger Rds., Box 2246, **Framingham,** MA 01701. (508) 875-5233

Grotonwood, **Groton,** MA 01450. (508) 448-5763

Marian Center, Inc., 1365 Northampton St., **Holyoke,** MA 01040. (413) 533-7171

Mount Marie Conference Center, Lower Westfield Rd., **Holyoke,** MA 01040. (413) 536-0853

National Shrine of Our Lady of La Salette, 315 Topsfield Rd., **Ipswich,** MA 01938. (508) 356-3266

Order of St. Anne, 18 Cambridge Turnpike, **Lincoln,** MA 01773 (617) 259-9800

New England Keswick Youth Camp, Adult Conference and Retreat Center, Chestnut Hill Rd., P.O. Box 156, **Monterey,** MA 01245. (413) 528-3604

Briarwood Conference Center, Shore Rd., P.O. Box 315, **Monument Beach,** MA. (508) 759-3476

Osgood Hill Conference Center, **North Andover,** MA 01845. (508) 682-7072

Rolling Ridge Conference Center, 666 Great Pond Rd., **North Andover,** MA 01845. (508) 682-8815

St. Joseph's Convent, 27 Mount Pleasant St. North, **North Brookfield,** MA 01535. (508) 867-6811

St. Joseph's Hall, 800 Tucker Rd., **North Dartmouth,** MA 02747. (508) 996-2413

Holy Cross Fathers Retreat, 824 Tucker Rd., **North Dartmouth,** MA 02747. (508) 993-2238

Holy Cross Fathers Retreat House, 409 Washington St., **North Easton,** MA 02356. (508) 238-2051

Foyer of Charity, 74 Hollett St., **North Scituate,** MA 02060. (617) 545-1080

The Community of Jesus, Inc., 5 Bay View Dr., Box 1094, **Orleans,** MA 02653. (508) 255-1094

St. Scholastica, Main St., **Petersham,** MA 01366. (508) 724-3213

Rowe Camp and Conference Center, Kings Highway Rd., **Rowe,** MA 01367. (413) 339-4216

Salvation Army, Hillcrest Conference Center, 10 Capen Hill Rd., **Sharon,** MA 02067. (617) 784-8924

Vipassana Meditation Center, P.O. Box 24, **Shelburne Falls,** MA 01370. (413) 625-2160

Calvary Retreat Center, 59 South Street, **Shrewsbury,** MA 01545. (508) 842-8821.

Sirius Community, Baker Rd., **Shutesbury,** MA 01072. (413) 259-1251

Temenos, P.O. Box 84A, Star Route, **Shutesbury,** MA 01072. (508) 544-6500

Camp Blairhaven, Howland's Landing, **South Duxbury,** MA 02332. (617) 837-6144. Mailing address: Massachusetts New Church Union, 175 Newbury St., Boston MA 02116.

Mary House, North Spencer Rd., P.O. Box 29, **Spencer,** MA 01562.

Memorial House Center for Spiritual Direction, 277 Carew St., **Springfield,** MA 01104. (413) 734-8843

Packard Manse, P.O. Box 450, **Stoughton,** MA 02072. (617) 344-9634

Espousal Retreat and Conference Center, 554 Lexington St., **Waltham,** MA 02154. (617) 893-3465

St. Joseph's Convent, 5 Maynard St., **Webster,** MA 01570. (508) 943-0467

Stump Sprouts Lodge, West Hill Rd., **West Hawley,** MA 01339. (413) 339-4265

Mother of Sorrows Retreat House, 110 Monastery Ave., P.O. Box 150, **West Springfield,** MA 01089. (413) 736-5458

Passionist Retreat and Conference Center, 110 Monastery Ave., **West Springfield,** MA 01089. (413) 736-5458

Genesis Spiritual Life Center, 53 Mill St., **Westfield,** MA 01085. (413) 562-3627

Campion Renewal Center, 319 Concord Rd., **Weston,** MA 02193. (617) 894-3199

Esther House of Spiritual Renewal, 783 Grove St., **Worcester,** MA 01605. (508) 757-6053

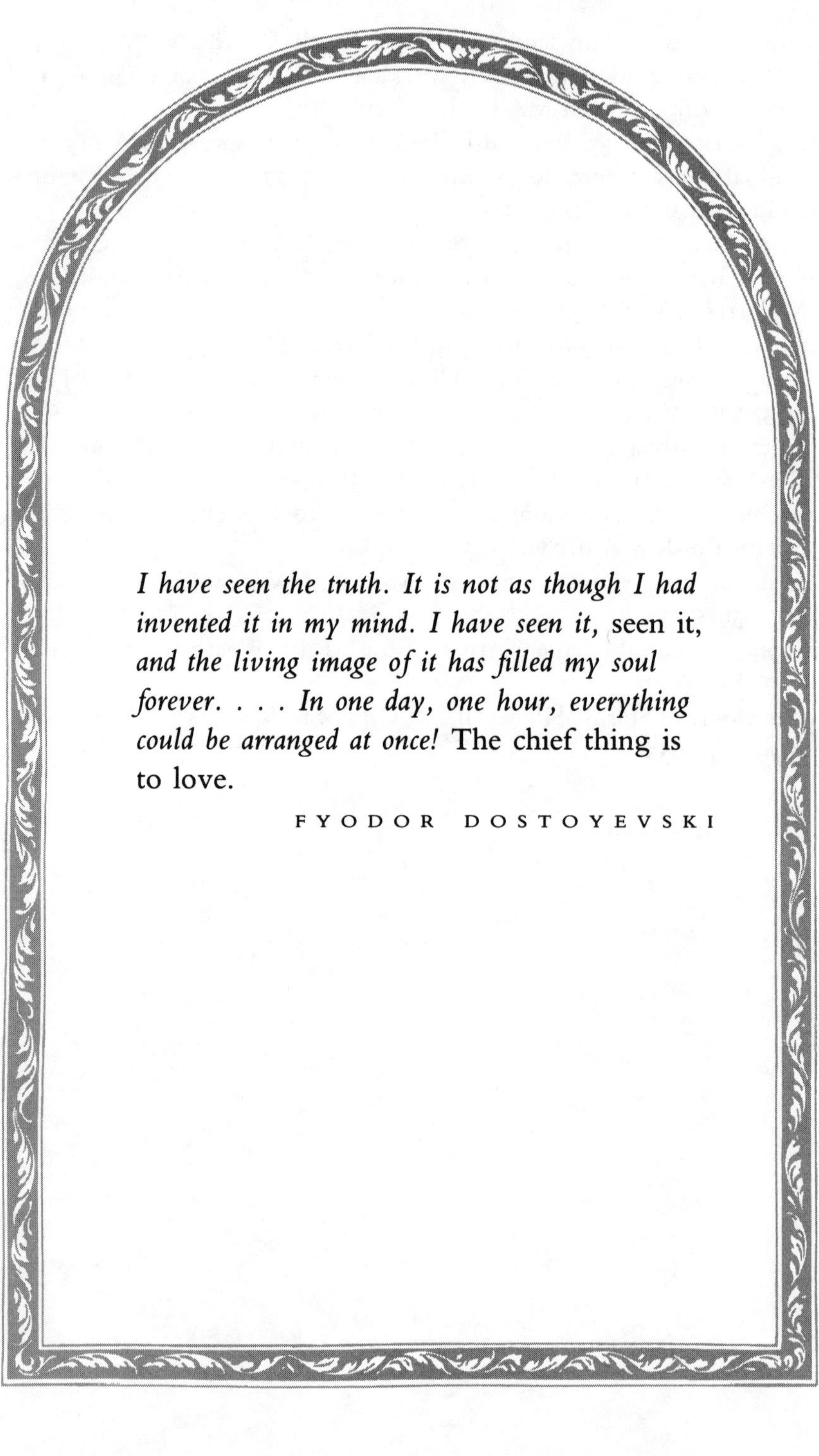

I have seen the truth. It is not as though I had invented it in my mind. I have seen it, seen it, *and the living image of it has filled my soul forever. . . . In one day, one hour, everything could be arranged at once!* The chief thing is to love.

FYODOR DOSTOYEVSKI

New Hampshire

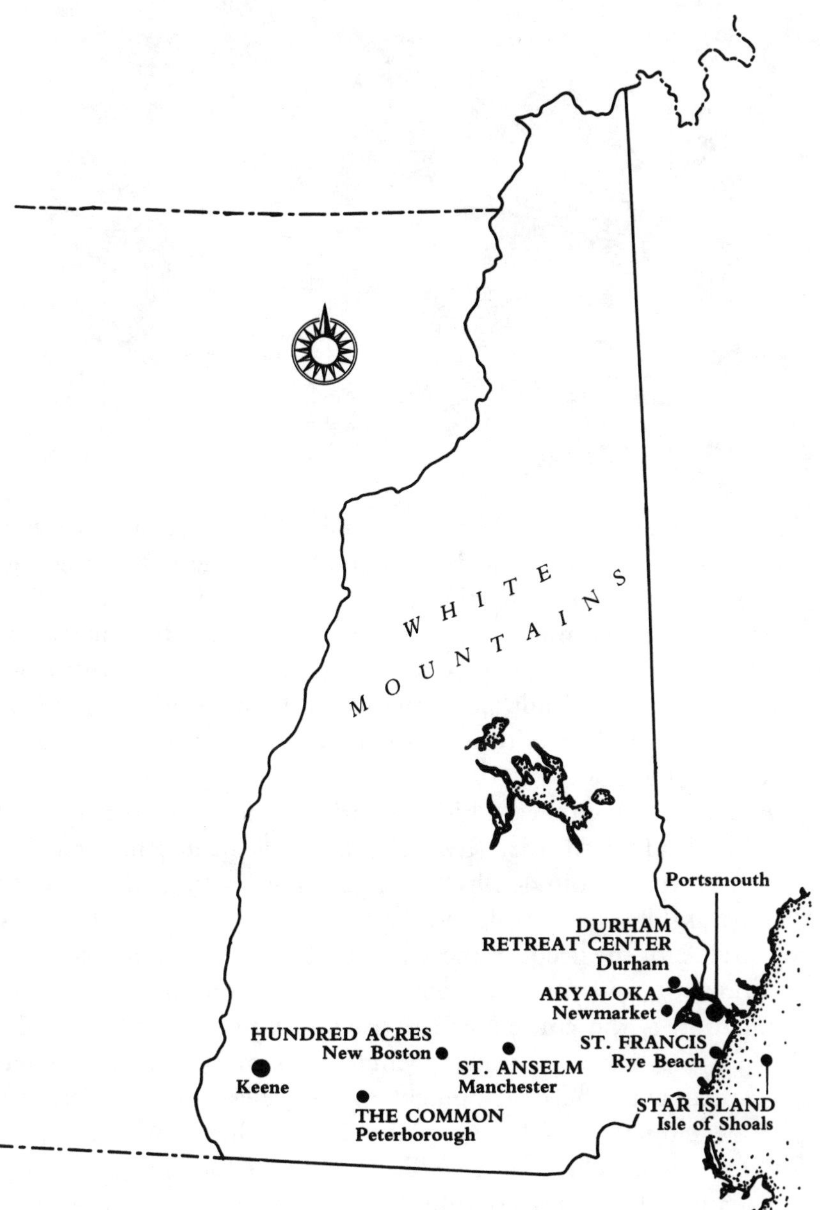

Aryaloka

Newmarket, NH

Aryaloka is a small Buddhist retreat and study center tucked away in a thicket of New England bushes and trees. The main building is constructed of two connecting geodesic domes, one side the living quarters of the community, and the other the meditation hall and meeting rooms. The property was acquired in the mid-1980s from a craftsman who had built the domes for his family's personal use. The design and execution of the doors make one appreciate how elegantly wood can be worked with.

Aryaloka (which means Noble World) is run by the Friends of the Western Buddhist Order (FWBO), which is an international Buddhist movement founded by an Englishman in 1967. The founder, Sangharakshita, has developed the practice and study of Buddhism to provide for the needs of those in the West who wish to explore the traditions of, and commit themselves to, the Buddhist way of life. Meditation is the cornerstone of Buddhist practice, and Aryaloka teaches two basic techniques: Mindfulness of Breathing, which is concerned with the development of awareness and concentration; and Development of Universal Loving-Kindness, which helps to foster positive feelings of friendliness and love for all human beings.

Each member of the community must contribute in some way to the group by working in the woodshop or performing household tasks or grounds maintenance. Each person also has a financial commitment to meet, and some do outside work such as carpentry and renovations.

Aryaloka offers classes in meditation, t'ai chi ch'uan, yoga, and Buddhist studies. Regular retreats are scheduled, as well as visitors' days, which offer an opportunity to meet the people involved and just look around.

There is a beautiful meditation hall on the top floor, and various niches where one can sit quietly to read and reflect. The community comes together at mealtimes to share vegetarian dishes. There are footpaths cleared around the 13 acres of surrounding property, so one can enjoy the clear New Hampshire air.

Aryaloka
Friends of the Western Buddhist Order
Heartwood Circle
Newmarket, NH *03857*
(603) 659-5456

Accommodations: *4 guest rooms for men and women, with a 2-day minimum stay; vegetarian meals with the community; daily meditation; study, work, walks on property; open year-round; $30 a day.*

Directions: *Newmarket is 70 miles north of Boston and 15 miles from Portsmouth, New Hampshire. From the north, take I-95 to Rte. 101 West, then Rte. 108 North toward Newmarket. From the south, take I-95 to Rte. 51 West, then Rte. 108 North to Newmarket. From Manchester, take Rte. 101 East to Rte. 125 North (left off the exit ramp), then Rte. 155. Turn right at the junction of Rte. 155 with Rte. 152.*

The Common
Peterborough, NH

In 1738, ten acres of this hilltop were designated as the site of the Peterborough town center or common, but the town grew in the valley below and eventually the property became a private farm. In 1898 it was acquired by the Cheney family, who built an imposing mansion with an outdoor pool and tennis court. In the 1950s it became a girls' school, and then in 1966 it was bought by the Carmelites for use as a seminary, and converted into a retreat center in 1968.

The mansion has been lovingly restored, with beautiful guest rooms. The main floor has two chapels, conference rooms, a large dining room off the kitchen, and a study that displays historical information about the mansion and the surrounding area. Carved into the fireplace mantel in the dining room is the following message: "They eat, they drink and in common sweet—Quaff immortality and Joy."

The center has splendid views to the west and southwest, looking across a valley to Mount Monadnock, which reportedly was climbed by both Thoreau and Emerson. Beyond the tennis court and pool is the cemetery that Thornton Wilder used as a setting for his play *Our Town.*

The three priests and two brothers who give retreats and care for the property live in a separate monastery a short distance from the mansion. The library below their quarters is available for guests' use in the afternoon. It is an inviting space, with beamed ceilings and comfortable chairs.

The Common is a retreat center for people and groups of all beliefs. There are retreats scheduled regularly throughout the year, and private retreatants are welcome. The Carmelites are available for consultation. There are 173 acres of woods and meadows that make up the grounds. Two hermitages are available, set apart from the other buildings.

Traditionally, New Englanders gathered at the common to share dreams and concerns. It seems fitting that Carmelites, named for hermits who lived on Mount Carmel in Palestine, should be living on this mountain, ministering to those who are on their own spiritual journeys.

The Common
174 Old Street Rd.
Peterborough, NH 03458
(603) 924-6060 (Mon.–Fri., 9 A.M.–1 P.M.)

Accommodations: *18 lovely bedrooms for 33 men and women; good community meals in the dining room; mass, morning and evening prayer; tennis court, swimming pool, 173 acres for hiking; open year-round except during the week of preparations for "The Faire," a Sunday-after-Labor-Day event; $85 a weekend.*

Directions: *Take Rte. 101 to the junction of Rte. 123 on the east side of Peterborough at the yellow blinking light.* Do not *follow Rte. 123, however; instead, drive north on Old Street Rd. for 1 mile. An oval sign reading* THE COMMON *hangs in the woods on the left; turn left into the woods. If you reach Peterborough on Rte. 202, turn east on Rte. 101 and follow the preceding instructions.*

Durham Retreat Center
Durham, NH

In the mid-1980s the former directors of a Sufi community felt that it was time to change their life-style so that they could spend more time with their children. They bought a parcel of land and built a three-level house designed so that family life could be separate from the five retreat rooms and large conference/meditation room on the first floor. The rooms are simple but comfortable. Meals are non-dairy vegetarian. Relevant books and a tape library are available.

The staff provides guided retreats and also trains retreat guides following the precepts of the Sufi Order and the teachings of Pir Vilayat Inayat Khan, a teacher known for integrating spiritual practice with modern psychology.

The retreat does not require an affiliation or interest in the Sufi Order, but is offered as a service to those seeking to develop their spiritual understanding. To demonstrate the point, the director quotes Thomas Merton: "We do not go into the desert to escape people but to learn how to find them; we do not leave them in order to have nothing more to do with them, but to find out how to do them the most good."

As Muhammad said, we are or can be identified with God by means of a beatific vision through which we become absorbed in God. Moslem mysticism has had a long and intricate history, and the Sufis were ascetics. Despite their intent to stay aloof from society, they did influence Moslem thinking by their ideals. Sufi poetry, such as *The Rubaiyat of Omar Khayyám,* has become world-renowned.

The purpose of a retreat here is to lift the veils covering the layers of cherished ideas, so that people may become aware of a sense of quality. If they are in confusion, they may find insight. They can learn how to begin to be true to themselves and compassionate toward others. They can experience a deep sense of inner peace as they rediscover the balance between relaxation and activity. Take the time to step back, then leap forward.

Durham Retreat Center
33 Demeritt Rd.
Durham, NH 03824
(603) 659-6708

Accommodations: *5 retreat rooms and 1 cabin for men and women on silent retreat; vegetarian meals are taken in rooms; daily meeting with retreat director; open year-round; $35 a night. Write for reservations and directions.*

Hundred Acres Monastery
New Boston, NH

In 1964 Father Paul Fitzgerald came from the Trappist Monastery at Spencer, Massachusetts, and founded Hundred Acres to fulfill a desire for a simpler life. The main building, which contains charming guest rooms, dining facilities, a living room, sitting rooms, and a chapel is a classic New England farmhouse, with low ceilings; generous, rambling rooms; and many fireplaces.

The monks have their quarters in the barn, a short distance from the main house. This building also serves as a library and a reading and study area. The large, open space is finished in natural wood paneling and lined with shelves of books making it an inviting, warm place. On either side of the main entrance are stairs that lead up to the monks' cells. To the right of the entrance is a nook with fireplace, sofa, and comfortable chairs for reading.

The community and guests have dinner together at 6 P.M. Guests are expected to structure their own time and help themselves to breakfast, lunch, and snacks, which are put out in the kitchen. They also take care of their own rooms and laundry, and are welcome to help with the many tasks needed to preserve the tranquillity of an orderly, clean home. The focus of the work at Hundred Acres is increasingly toward the care of the environment.

There is a simple mass every evening at 7, usually celebrated in the living room. The 80-year-old abbot sits in a chair, his altar a coffee table. Far removed from ecclesiastical pomp and ceremony, it seems the very essence of religious worship and community.

There is a large lawn behind the main house and a covered patio off the kitchen, a lovely place where guests can sit. Down the road is Scobie Pond, also known as Haunted Lake because of the sounds the ice makes as it cracks each winter. Visitors can go for long walks around the lake, a beautiful, clean 160 acres of fairly shallow water. There is a public beach for swimming and sunbathing by day or, in the evening, for moon-watching and stargazing.

Hundred Acres Monastery
***New Boston, NH** 03070*
(603) 487-2638

Accommodations: *The original farmhouse houses 8–10 men, women, and children with singles for a few extra men in the "barn"; family-style dining with the community; evening mass in the living room at 7 P.M. (Sundays at 9:30 A.M.); 169 acres with a lovely lake down the quiet road; open year-round; suggested donation: $25 a night, with special rates for extended stays.*

Directions: *Located 30 miles west of Manchester, NH, and 3 miles outside New Boston off Rte. 136 West (the road to Francetown and Peterborough). From Rte. 101, take the Bedford exit, left lane to Rte. 114. Follow Rte. 114 to the end, and turn left at the light to Goffstown. Take Rte. 13 to New Boston; turn right at the general store to Rte. 136; 3 miles on the left is a big sign on a tree, reading 100 ACRES; turn left and follow the paved road 3/10 mile to a dirt road; bear right at the lake.*

St. Anselm Abbey
Manchester Priory
Manchester, NH

In 1889 the Benedictines came to New Hampshire and established a monastery and school on 300 acres of high ground overlooking the town of Manchester. The school is a liberal arts college with an enrollment now close to 2,000 students. The grounds are exceptionally well maintained, with expansive lawns leading up to the main buildings. The most prominent is the Abbey-College Church, which is connected to the monastery. The 35 to 40 monks who live here assemble daily in the splendid chapel to sing the canonical hours.

In the Benedictine tradition, they are self-supporting from the school and make rooms available for retreatants. Men are accommodated in the monastery, where they are expected to follow the routine of the monks; the hallways are hushed, the monks' cells comfortable but plain. There are large, arched windows surrounding a silent courtyard in which one catches an occasional glimpse of a cowled monk. Women are housed with the Sisters of St. Benedict in Manchester Priory, a separate building a few hundred yards across the road from the monastery. The nuns provide a quiet, homey, and comfortable setting for their guests, with family-style meals served in the dining room. They have a small chapel, but go across the road to attend services at the monastery. At the monastery noon meal there is a *lectio* (Latin for "reading"), during which one can reflect on the words read.

The aim of the Benedictine rule is to devote every aspect of one's life to the service of God, and the atmosphere at St. Anselm is indeed one of active prayer.

St. Anselm Abbey
Manchester Priory
Manchester, NH 03102
(603) 669-1030 (Abbey)
(603) 622-6296 (Priory)

Accommodations: *Men, with a recommendation, are welcome for private retreats in the monastery itself as rooms are available; up to 8 women can stay across the road at Manchester Priory; men eat in silence with the monks; women have home-cooked meals, family-style, with the nuns; canonical hours are sung by a choir of 35–40 in a beautiful chapel; 300 acres of campus, woods, trails; college library and facilities; open year-round; free-will donation.*

Directions: *The abbey and priory are located 50 miles north of Boston. From I-93 North to Rte. 293 North, exit left to Rte. 101 West (Bedford/Goffstown). At junction of Rtes. 101 and 114, take Rte. 114 North. Continue through the traffic lights (mini-golf and restaurant on right) to Saint Anselm's Drive. Turn right onto the drive. The campus is approximately 1 mile on the right.*

St. Francis Retreat Center

Rye Beach, NH

Just a short walk from the 18-mile stretch of New Hampshire coastline between Maine and Massachusetts is an imposing, Tudor-style structure built in 1919 as the Stoneleigh Manor Hotel. During the 1930s the hotel operated as a women's college until the beginning of World War II, when it served as an air academy until 1945. During this period, the story goes, the elevator was torn out and melted down for bullets. The Franciscans acquired the buildings in 1950 and used the property as a seminary until 1973. Then it served as the local parish church, but when, in 1979, a new church was opened nearby, the mission of the retreat center officially began.

The spirit of hospitality for which the Franciscans are noted is evident in the friendliness and enthusiasm of the staff. Many of the hotel furnishings were acquired with the purchase, and one of the brothers, who has been living here for 30 years, has dedicated his woodworking skills to restoring and maintaining the furniture and the original wood paneling.

Retreatants are housed in double and single rooms. There are four conference areas, a large dining room operated by lay professionals, a library, and a chapel where mass is said daily. The lounge on the lower level, where coffee and tea are always available, leads to the grounds and several patios and sitting areas.

As many as 8,000 people come each year and stay for periods

ranging from a few days to as long as a month. The center offers weekend retreats dealing with alcoholism, single parenthood, and separation and divorce. There are also week-long retreats focusing on spiritual values. Private retreatants are welcome at any time, even during formal retreats.

"The Hermitage," a separate building with its own living and dining rooms, chapel, and ten single bedrooms, offers a group the opportunity to experience solitude in the context of community. Retreatants spend time in silence, but gather during the day for prayer, liturgy, silent meals, and evening faith-sharing sessions.

The center is on six acres of beautifully landscaped grounds just across a road from a private golf course. In less than ten minutes one can wander to the ocean, where there is a two-mile boardwalk. The comfortable atmosphere of the old hotel, its beautiful grounds and fresh, bracing ocean air, and the spiritual work now taking place, all contribute to an extraordinary sense of renewal.

St. Francis Retreat Center
860 Central Rd.
***Rye Beach, NH** 03871*
(603) 964-5559

Accommodations: *For men and women, 54 doubles and 20 singles plus a 10-room hermitage; tasty buffet-style meals; morning mass; 6 acres of landscaped gardens, 2 1/2 miles of boardwalk on the ocean, 1 block away; excellent book and gift shop; closed first 2 weeks of September; $37 a night.*

Directions: *Rye Beach is on the New Hampshire seacoast, 55 miles north of Boston. From I-95, take New Hampshire Exit 1 (Seabrook). Turn right at the exit, proceed to the traffic lights, and turn left onto U.S. 1. Drive 6 1/2 miles, through Hampton Center, to a set of traffic lights at the Village Shopping Center. Turn right onto Rte. 101D, and follow Rte. 101D 3 miles to the ocean. Turn left onto Rte. 1A and proceed for about 1 mile to Central Rd., marked by a modern brick hotel on the corner. Turn left onto Central Rd. The retreat center is the fifth building on the right.*

Star Island

Isle of Shoals, NH

To reach Star Island, you take a ferry from Portsmouth for the ten-mile, one-hour ride to the 1 1/2-square-mile Isle of Shoals. The remote isle was acquired in 1915 by a Unitarian organization, and dedicated "to the brotherhood of all earnest souls, to the untrammeled study and utterance of the truth, to the promotion of pure religion."

There are weekend or week-long conferences and retreats scheduled from mid-June to mid-September and open to everybody. These are generally of a spiritual nature, and most are Unitarian Universalist–oriented. There are also some that deal with nature study, since the island is rich in bird life and the shoreline is unspoiled. One week is an Elderhostel.

Most visitors stay in the main building, a former hotel. Small cottages and other outbuildings are comfortable but rustic. Each floor has toilet facilities but no baths. Owing to the limited water supply, showers are available only twice a week. Electricity is also limited, and visitors are discouraged from using electrical appliances such as hair dryers and electric razors.

Meals are served family-style in a communal dining room. Children's programs are available during adult activities. There is a snack bar open daily, as well as a book and gift shop. The one telephone may be used only for emergency calls.

Each evening, "shoalers" (as regular conference attendees are called) carrying candle lanterns form a procession and walk up to the chapel, which is the highest point on the island. The lanterns are hung inside during the ensuing service and provide the only light. Silence is observed while ascending and descending the hill.

There is much to explore along the shoreline, from the marine gardens on the east side to Lover's Cave at the south tip. This rustic island retreat is secluded yet well organized, with a warm sense of community.

Star Island
P.O. Box 178, Isle of Shoals
Portsmouth, NH 03801
(603) 964-7252
Winter: *110* ***Arlington St.***
Boston, MA *02116*
(617) 426-7988

Accommodations: *Former hotel houses 250 men, women, and children for summer programs (register by March to ensure attendance); healthful, family-style meals in a community dining room; candlelight chapel services each evening; 2 naturalists on staff; programming for children; 1 1/2-square-mile island for summer activities; open mid-June to mid-September; $226–$238 average a week for adults, plus 15-percent gratuity for staff "Pelicans."*

Directions: *From I-95, take Exit 7 (Portsmouth), North or South, and follow signs to Downtown Portsmouth/Isle of Shoals Ferry. The dock is about 1/2 mile from the exit, on the left. For more boat information, contact:*

The Isle of Shoals Steamship Company
P.O. Box 311
Portsmouth, NH 03801
(603) 431-5500

New Hampshire: Other Places

Geneva Point Center, Star Route 62, P.O. Box 469, **Center Harbor,** NH 03226. (603) 253-4366

Deering Conference Center, RFD 1, P.O. Box 138, Rte. 149, **Deering,** NH 03244. (603) 529-2311

La Salette Shrine and Conference Center, P.O. Box 369, **Enfield,** NH 03748. (603) 632-7087

Oblate Retreat House, 200 Lowell Rd., **Hudson,** NH 03051. (603) 882-8141

Joseph House, 279 Cartier St., **Manchester,** NH 03102. (603) 627-9493

Sisters of the Precious Blood, 700 Bridge St., **Manchester,** NH 03104. (603) 623-4264

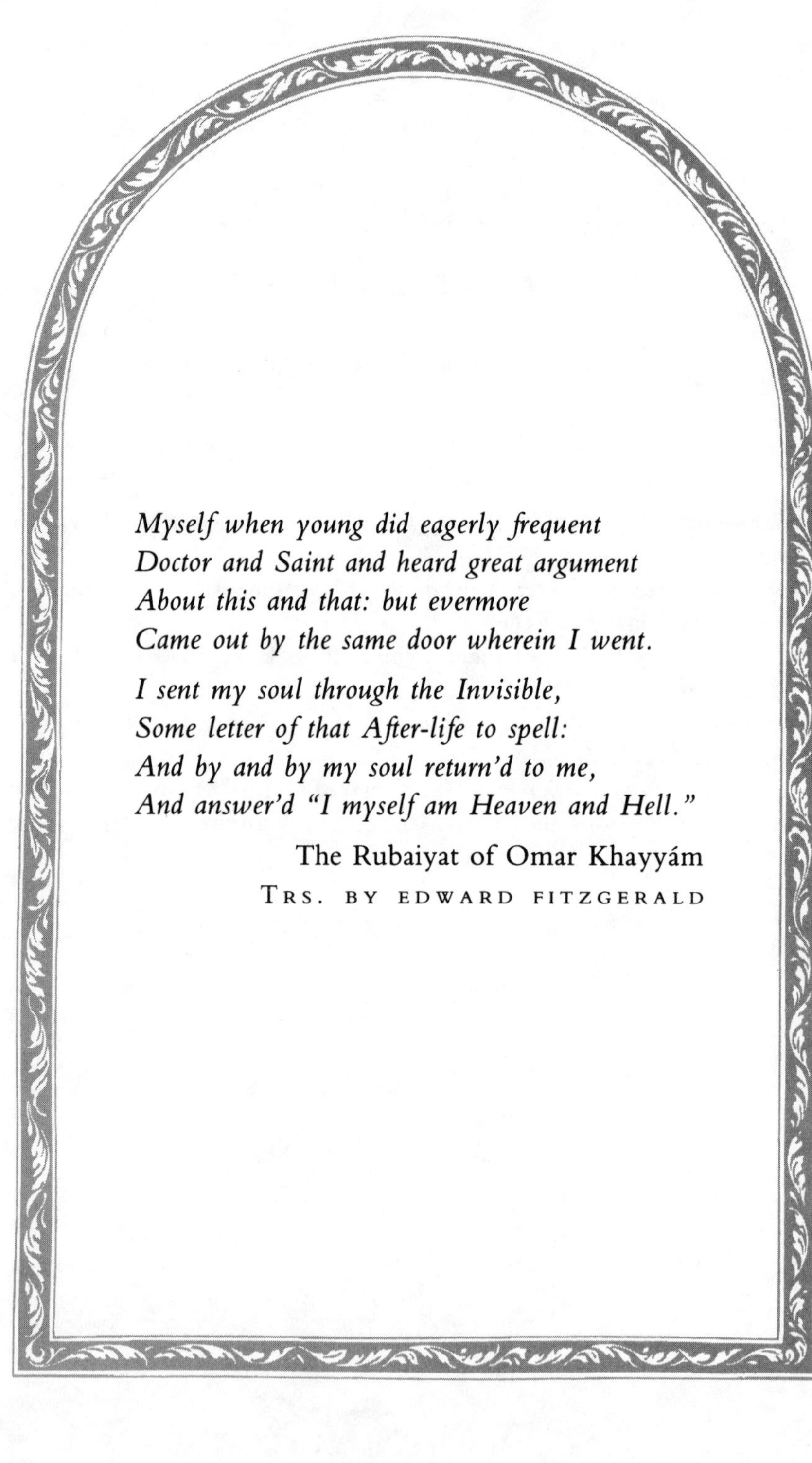

Myself when young did eagerly frequent
Doctor and Saint and heard great argument
About this and that: but evermore
Came out by the same door wherein I went.

I sent my soul through the Invisible,
Some letter of that After-life to spell:
And by and by my soul return'd to me,
And answer'd "I myself am Heaven and Hell."

The Rubaiyat of Omar Khayyám
TRS. BY EDWARD FITZGERALD

New Jersey

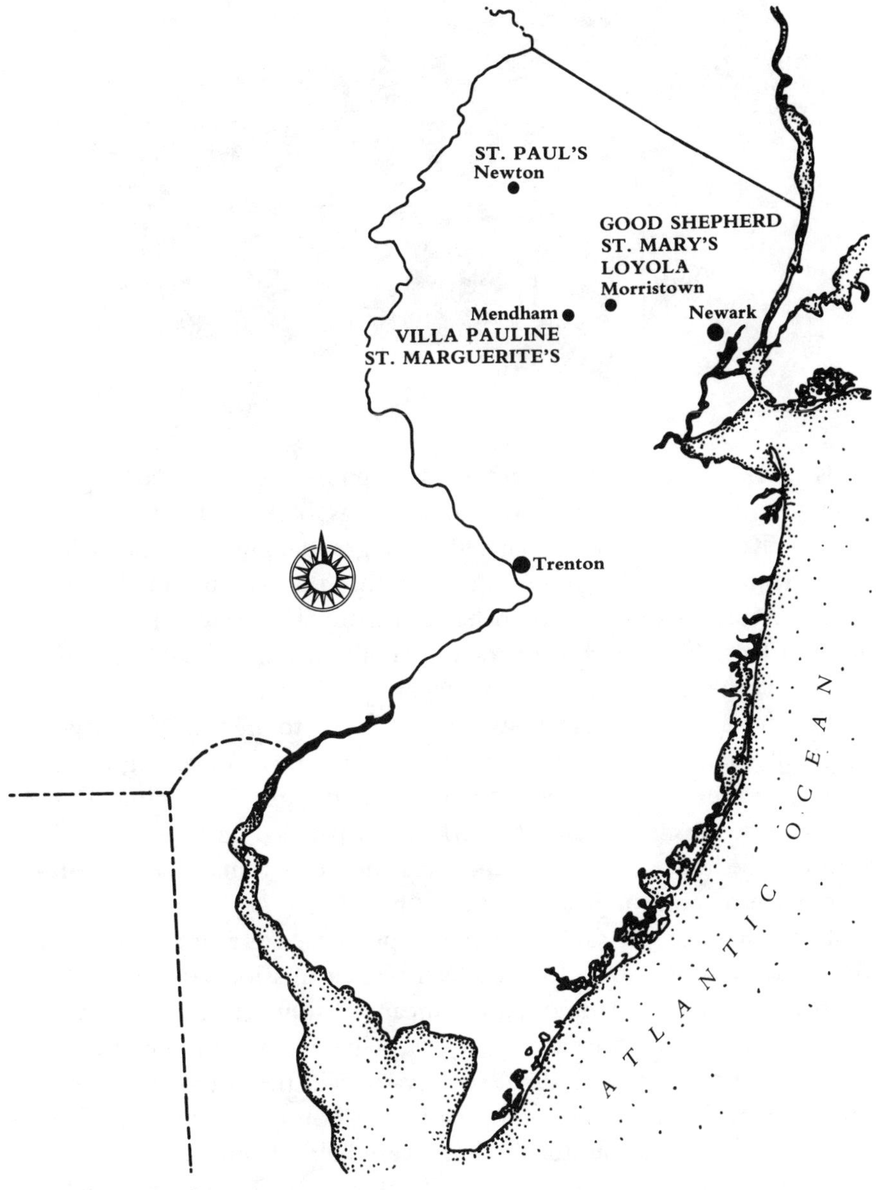
ST. PAUL'S
Newton
GOOD SHEPHERD
ST. MARY'S
LOYOLA
Morristown
Mendham
Newark
VILLA PAULINE
ST. MARGUERITE'S
Trenton
ATLANTIC OCEAN

Good Shepherd Center
Morristown, NJ

This brick manor house, with its sweeping views of Washington Valley and the Watchung Mountains, was built in 1904–1905 by Gustav Kissel, who was married to a granddaughter of Cornelius Vanderbilt. The house was designed so that a private polo field—the first in Morris County—could be seen from the terrace. The lawns and gardens, filled with flowers and an abundance of wildlife, provide a wonderful setting for quiet contemplation.

The mansion, with its freestanding staircase to the third floor, was originally named Wheatsheaf House. The railings and ceiling moldings have the wheat symbol as part of the design. The living room has become the chapel, and the dark wood-paneled library—the only room in the house where smoking was allowed—remains a comfortable place to read or just to sit and think.

The Sisters of the Good Shepherd purchased the property from the Kissel family in 1951 for a convent. Their mission was to care for orphans. Since they had no regular means of support, they would go to the local churches each Sunday to beg for alms for the ensuing week. In 1971, as the needs of society shifted, the sisters responded by transforming the building into a retreat house where some of the earliest marriage encounter sessions were held. There is now a regular series of retreats, in keeping with their order's mission of helping others in pain. The nuns have welcomed battered and abused women and those recently released from jail.

The sisters have done a splendid job of preserving the charm of the old mansion. The rooms are clean and attractive. The tasty meals are buffet or family-style, according to group size. There is a swimming pool on the 11 acres of grounds, and the property is just across the road from Foster Fields, with its old-fashioned farming and garden plots for interested youngsters.

At 7:45 A.M. each day, mass is said by a Benedictine priest from nearby St. Mary's Abbey, and this is followed by breakfast and morning prayer. The three resident sisters are gracious and relaxed as they care for their guests. As their brochure says, "Teach me to sit still, to think, to pray so that when there is something to do, I may do it with clear sight, with energy, with effectiveness, and maybe with a little more love."

Good Shepherd Center
74 ***Kahdena Rd.***
Morristown, NJ *07960*
(201) 538-4233

Accommodations: *Beds for 48 men and women in comfortable single and double mansion rooms; home-cooked meals are served buffet or family style; mass daily; swimming pool, terraced gardens, abundant bird life; across the road, Foster Fields, a lovely, old-fashioned working farm, is open to visitors; open year-round; costs vary.*

Directions: *From I-80, take I-287 South to the exit for Madison Avenue and Rte. 24/Morristown. Turn right at the end of the ramp and right again at the traffic light onto Rte. 24 West through the center of town, around Morristown Square, and back onto 24 West for 1 mile past the Burnham Park swimming pools (on the left). Turn right onto Kahdena Road (there is a Foster Fields sign here), and take the first right into Good Shepherd Driveway, between brick pillars, to top of drive.*

Loyola House of Retreats

Morristown, NJ

In 1925 a retreatant asked a staff member of a Staten Island retreat center, "Why not a Jesuit retreat house in New Jersey?" And so, in 1927, with the approval of the Newark diocese, Father Herman Storck found a suitable property. Built in 1904 by a wealthy banker, this 44-room Georgian revival mansion of Indiana limestone and brick originally had 36 bedrooms and 15 baths. The interior woodwork of carved walnut is still meticulously cared for. Many pieces of oversized furniture have been donated by retreatants and fit well in the spacious rooms. Wings were added in 1949 and 1957, and a new chapel in 1963, all in keeping with the original design, so that it now has the proportions and look of Buckingham Palace. Just inside the main entrance is a plaque honoring Welcome Bender, who donated the property to the Jesuits by handing the deed to his 12-year-old son, who in turn presented it with a formal bow to Father Storck.

The sixty-plus-year history of Loyola is a mirror of Catholic church history as its records trace the steady rise of retreat groups and attendance through the late 1920s and 1930s. Numbers declined during the 1940s as young men went off to serve in World War II, then increased in the 1950s to a peak in 1963. The difficult years were 1966 to 1980, when spiritual interest waned, but the 1980s appear to have seen a spiritual reawakening.

Many groups and individuals feel that Loyola is a "home away from home," and come annually for their weekend of spiritual renewal. It was here that in 1942 two members of AA met and conceived the idea of a special retreat group for recovering alcoholics, and took as their patron Matt Talbot, a Dublin laborer with a reputation for sanctity. The first Matt Talbot retreat was held here in 1943, and now the movement has spread far and wide.

There is a staff of 12 to administer a full schedule of weekend retreats for men and women, days of prayer, midweek meetings, and private retreats. They also serve parish councils and parish societies, as well as schoolchildren, and will adapt a program to fit the needs of a particular group. Private retreatants are also welcome.

The 30 acres of beautifully tended grounds with outdoor Stations of the Cross and the impressive mansion, as one staff member describes it, provide "space, scripture, and silence."

Loyola House of Retreats
161 James St.
***Morristown, NJ** 07960*
(201) 539-0740

Accommodations: *Mansion has 85 private rooms for men and women; family-style or buffet meals; mass daily; 30 acres of lawn, gardens, woodlands, paths, swimming pool; free-will offering for silent weekend and midweek retreats for laypeople; varying fees for other programs; open year-round.*

Directions: *From I-80, take I-287 south to Exit 29 (Harter St.). Follow signs to James St. nearby, and turn left on James St. Watch for Loyola sign on left.*

St. Marguerite's Retreat House
Mendham, NJ

The Episcopalian nuns of the Community of St. John Baptist came to the United States from England in 1874. Their rule is based on the Augustinian tradition of combining active work with contemplative prayer. The rambling brick building that is now St. Marguerite's Retreat House was once an orphanage that the nuns administered for almost 40 years. In 1960 the house became a retreat and conference center used mainly by Episcopalian groups, but there are also some Methodists and Lutherans who return year after year. There is a fine professional cook in charge of the kitchen—a rare treat in such surroundings. The wood paneling and the generous bedrooms and meeting rooms bespeak 19th-century charm, so that one really does feel as though one has retreated from today's world.

Across the front lawn is the Convent of St. John Baptist, the home of the nine sisters who administer the retreat house. This impressive white French Gothic structure was built in 1916 and designed by a student of the architect Ralph Adams Crane. The charming interior of tile floors and stucco walls with deep inset windows has a distinctly southern-European flavor. There are beautiful religious artifacts throughout. The main chapel, with its arched ceiling, contains a perfect example of an umbrella pillar. There is another, smaller chapel on the second floor, where the sisters gather daily to pray a fivefold office beginning with Lauds at 6:30 A.M. and ending with Compline at 8:30 P.M.

Ninety-three acres of woodlands surround the buildings and deepen the sense of seclusion. There is a neatly kept graveyard, reminiscent of a European churchyard, near the drive at the side of the convent.

Private retreatants are always welcome at the convent, and take their meals with the nuns. This is a small community with a deep commitment to an interior life of prayer and devotion. The nuns work to "keep a sparkle in the community," as their foundress used to say, and to share the joy of religious life.

St. Marguerite's Retreat House
Convent of St. John Baptist
***P.O. Box** 240*
***Mendham, NJ** 07945*
(201) 543-4641

Accommodations: *Simple singles for 29 men and women; home-cooked buffet meals; prayer 5 times daily at the convent; 93 acres for walking; open Labor Day to mid-December, and January to mid-June; $45 a night.*

Directions: *From I-80, take I-287 South to the first Morristown exit. Proceed past the railway station to Park Ave. and the town square; go around 2 sides of the square and turn right on Rte. 24 West. Follow through 2 traffic lights in Mendham and continue 1/2 mile to a left turn into the entrance, marked by a sign. Bear right at the fork in the road, and continue past "The Steps" building to the end of the road. The retreat house is the large red brick mansion on the left, just beyond the white stucco convent.*

St. Mary's Abbey–Delbarton
Morristown, NJ

The former Kountze estate, Delbarton, was purchased in 1926 by Benedictine monks from Newark as a house of studies for its young monks. According to legend, another site was almost chosen, but the prior who favored Delbarton went there and planted Benedictine medals in the ground, convinced that once Saint Benedict had taken root there, he would guide the choice of the community. And, indeed, the final vote was for the 400-acre Kountze property. Through the late 1920s and the 1930s, the monks farmed the land and modified the 50-room mansion for their community's needs. The armor room was transformed into the chapel (swords into plowshares) and the music studio into the refectory. In those early years, the full-scale farm helped the monks become self-sufficient.

Then the bishop, concerned with the lack of Catholic schools in the diocese, urged the Benedictines to start a boy's prep school. The first 12 students matriculated in 1939. Since that time the number of students has grown to 500, and the farmland has been turned into playing fields for soccer, lacrosse, football, and baseball. The Delbarton School has become one of the most distinguished Catholic prep schools in the United States. The school has evolved into a day school, and a former dormitory is now used as a retreat house, particularly for graduating and confirmation classes of teenagers.

The back lawn of the mansion, now called Old Main, is an Italian garden with marble columns and statues; two of the latter, by Bernini, are now on loan to the Metropolitan Museum.

The growth of both the school and the community necessitated the building of a new abbey. This church—which can seat 700—reflects the spirit of the Benedictines; it is entered through huge portals defining the worship area and marking the passage into the temple of God. The circular floor slopes gradually toward the center, focusing attention on the altar and encouraging participation in the liturgy. The stark simplicity of the design is complemented by the Amish-made pews. The monks meet here daily for mass and to sing the canonical hours. Retreatants and guests are welcome.

Some private retreatants are accommodated in the monastery.  Meals are taken cafeteria-style with the monks, who have an excellent chef. The ordered prayer life of the community amid the spacious grounds makes this a very appealing place. On celebrating the opening of the new abbey church in 1966, one of the monks wrote, "You must in all things take your brother into account . . . never come to a halt; go forward with your brothers, run toward the goal in the footprints of Christ."

St. Mary's Abbey–Delbarton
270 Mendham Rd.
***Morristown, NJ** 07960*
(201) 538-3231

Accommodations: *For 64 men, women, and teenagers, 32 rooms in a modern retreat center on the grounds of a 100-year-old estate; delicious food served in the cafeteria; prayer 4 times daily in a stark chapel with Amish-made pews; orchards, tennis, playing fields, extensive property for walking; open year-round. Call for rates.*

Directions: *Take I-80 to I-287 South. Take Exit 29 (Harter Rd.) and follow Rte. 24 West through town, around the town square, and on past the Burnham Park swimming pools, on the left. Watch for St. Mary's Abbey–Delbarton on your left within a few minutes.*

St. Paul's Abbey
Queen of Peace Retreat House
Newton, NJ

St. Paul's Abbey, a Catholic Benedictine community just two hours from metropolitan New York, was founded in 1924 by a monk from the Archabbey of St. Ottilien in Bavaria. Over the years, monks from St. Paul's have established missions in Africa, South America, and the Far East. One room in the abbey is devoted to works of art brought back by these missionaries, and outside the chapel there are impressive African wooden sculptures.

The former monastery, a stately Normandy structure, has been transformed into the Queen of Peace Retreat House, where, on most weekends, the monks welcome parish groups, self-help organizations, and private retreatants, giving them a chance to share the calm and prayerful life here. About 3,000 people visit St. Paul's each year. The community itself now occupies the larger monastery that was built to replace the original building.

On the 500-acre property, there is a large evergreen and Christmas tree farm that produces thousands of trees for sale every year. In 1989 the monks planted 12,000 seedling replacements. The monks keep a large number of beehives, and the honey is sold in the gift shop, which also offers religious articles.

A walk down the road past the entrance leads into the woods and to a recreation field that borders a one-square-mile lake at the edge of the grounds.

St. Paul's Abbey
Queen of Peace Retreat House
***Newton, NJ** 07860*
(201) 383-2470 ***(monastery)***
(201) 383-0660 ***(retreat house)***

Accommodations: *60 singles and doubles for 85 men and women in the retreat house, and some rooms in the monastery; family-style meals; prayer 4 times daily; 500 acres, lake, woods, Christmas tree farm; open year-round; $30 per night, $65 per weekend.*

Directions: *From I-80, take Exit 25 (Rte. 206 North, Newton). Follow Rte. 206 North to the 107 mile post, and watch for the retreat house on the left within 1/2 mile.*

Villa Pauline
Mendham, NJ

Nestled in the Orange Mountains of Morris County, this 100-acre estate has an outstanding vista of the surrounding hills and woodlands. The 44-room Georgian mansion was built in 1892 by a former president of the New York Stock Exchange. Its wide porches open onto a colonnade that leads first to a pergola, then on to the Italian gardens graced with stone benches and English boxwood hedges.

In 1926 the property was acquired by the Catholic Sisters of Christian Charity, an order founded in Germany in the late 19th century. The sisters established schools and day-care centers, as well as ministering to blind children. Their activities were curtailed by Bismarck's anti-church policy, so the nuns came to America to continue their work. In the course of time, they bought this property to serve as headquarters for their eastern United States province. In the 1930s the new mother house and the Assumption College for Sisters were built nearby, and the mansion, renamed Villa Pauline after the sister who had founded the order, became a retreat and guesthouse.

The annual schedule is divided into a guest season, from mid-June to Labor Day, and a retreat season from Labor Day to early June. The guest season is open only to women wishing to spend a quiet vacation with the nuns. Women guests are also accommodated for long holiday weekends or weeks at Thanksgiving, Christmas, Easter, and Memorial Day weekend. Retreat weekends are conducted by a priest or other leader, and focus on personal prayer and solitude. During the week there are single days of recollection, usually for groups. The facilities are also open to organizations for their own spiritually oriented purposes.

There is daily mass at 7 A.M. at the impressive convent chapel nearby, just inside the main entrance to the college.

The sisters provide an atmosphere of peace and comfort, which enables guests to forget for a little while the demands of society and business, and experience a healthier approach to daily life.

Villa Pauline
Hilltop Rd.
***Mendham, NJ** 07945*
(201) 543-9058

Accommodations: *20 rooms for 50 people (predominantly women) in a Georgian mansion; hearty, home-cooked buffet meals served in a family dining room; mass daily; 100 hilltop acres; women invited for vacations at holiday times and during specified weeks in summer; open Labor Day to mid-June for weekend retreats; mid-June to Labor Day session includes guest vacation time; costs vary according to length of stay.*

Directions: *From I-80, take I-287 South to Exit 26B (Bernardsville). Turn left at the traffic light onto U.S. 202 South. At the center of Bernardsville, a flagpole stands in the center of a triangle. Bear right onto Rte. 525 (also known as Anderson Rd., Anderson Hill Rd., and Mendham Rd.). Continue on this road for 3 1/2 miles. The entrance sign is on the right.*

New Jersey: Other Places

St. Pius X House, P.O. Box 216, **Blackwood,** NJ 08012. (609) 227-1436

Jain Ashram, RD 4, P.O. Box 374, **Blairstown,** NJ 07824. (201) 362-9830

The Marianist, P.O. Box D-2, **Cape May Point,** NJ 08212. (609) 884-3829

Bethlehem Hermitage, Box 315, **Chester,** NJ 07930.

Xavier Center, **Convent Station,** NJ 07961. (201) 292-6488

Stella Maris Retreat House, 981 Ocean Ave., **Elberon,** NJ 07740. (201) 229-0602

Cenacle Retreat House, 411 River Rd., **Highland Park,** NJ 08904. (201) 249-8100

San Alfonso Retreat House, 755 Ocean Ave., **Long Branch,** NJ 07740. (201) 222-2731

Carmelite Retreat House, 1071 Ramapo Valley Rd., **Mahwah,** NJ 07430. (201) 327-7090

Francis House of Prayer, Box 1111, Springside Rd., **Mount Holly,** NJ 08060. (609) 871-1999

John Woolman Memorial House, 99 Branch St., **Mount Holly,** NJ 08060. (609) 267-3226

The Upper Room Spiritual Center, West Bangs Ave., Rte. 33, P.O. Box 1104, **Neptune,** NJ 07753. (201) 922-0550

St. Joseph's Villa, **Peapack,** NJ 07977. (201) 234-0334

Emmaus Retreat House, 101 Center St., **Perth Amboy,** NJ 08861. (201) 442-7688

Mount St. Francis Retreat Center, **Ringwood,** NJ 07456. (201) 962-9778

St. Joseph by the Sea, 400 Route 35 North, **South Mantoloking,** NJ 08738. (201) 892-8494

Trinity Center, 1292 Long Hill Rd., P.O. Box 205, **Stirling,** NJ 07080. (201) 647-7112

Villa Maria by the Sea Retreat House, **Stone Harbor,** NJ 08247. (609) 368-3621

Aldersgate Center, P.O. Box 122, **Swartswood,** NJ 07877. (201) 383-5978

Morningstar House of Prayer, 312 Upper Ferry Rd., **Trenton,** NJ 08628. (609) 882-2766

Mount Eden Retreat, PO Box 287, **Washington,** NJ 07882. (908) 782-2713 and 782-2702.

Tibetan Buddhist Learning Center, RD 1, Box 306A8, **Washington,** NJ 07882. (201) 689-6080

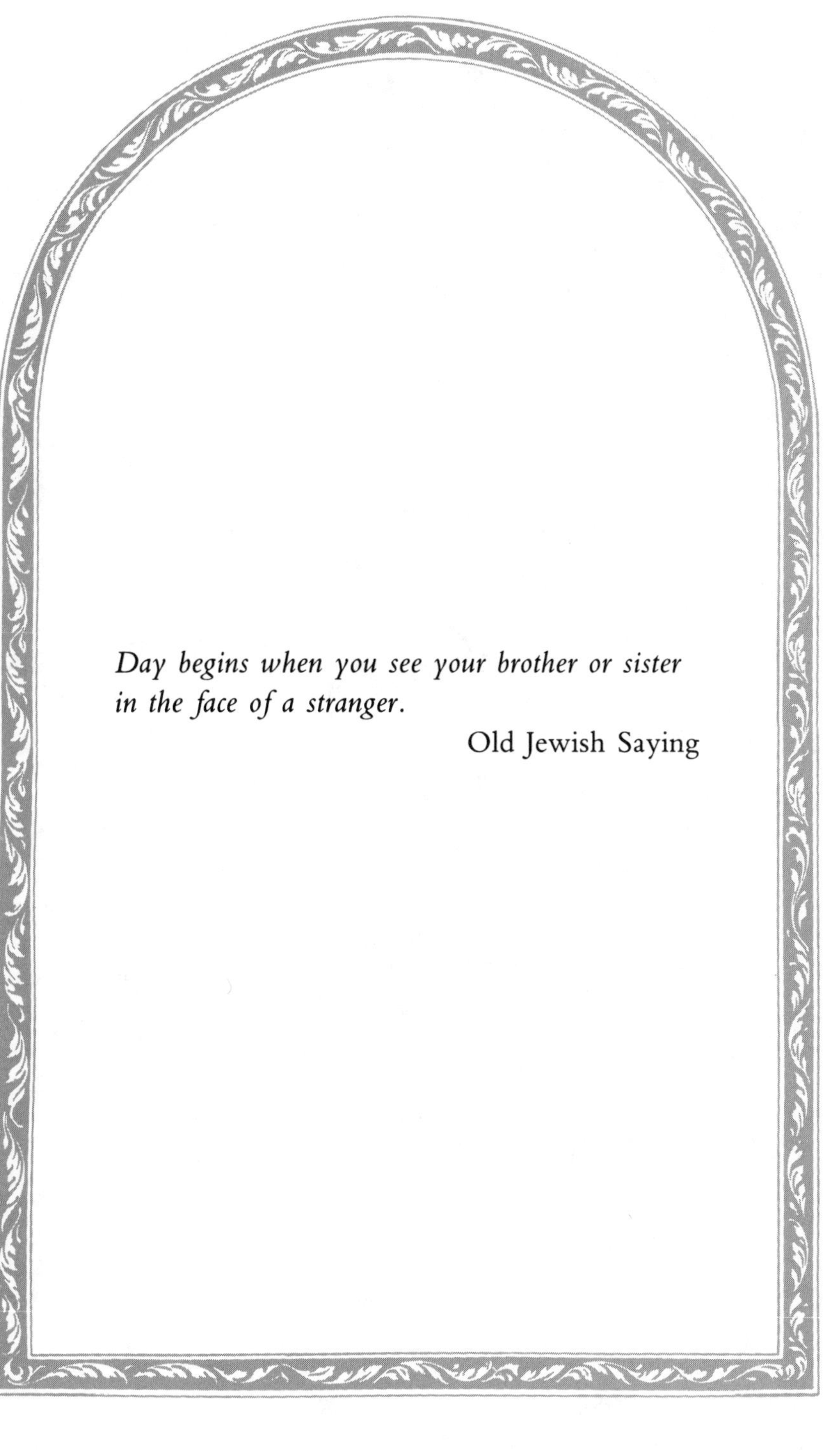

Day begins when you see your brother or sister in the face of a stranger.

Old Jewish Saying

New York

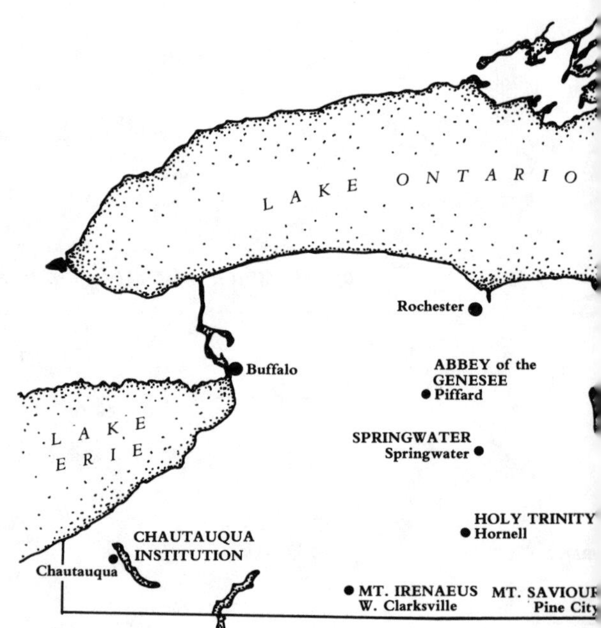
LAKE ONTARIO
Rochester
Buffalo
ABBEY of the
GENESEE
Piffard
LAKE
ERIE
SPRINGWATER
Springwater
HOLY TRINITY
Hornell
CHAUTAUQUA
INSTITUTION
Chautauqua
MT. IRENAEUS
W. Clarksville

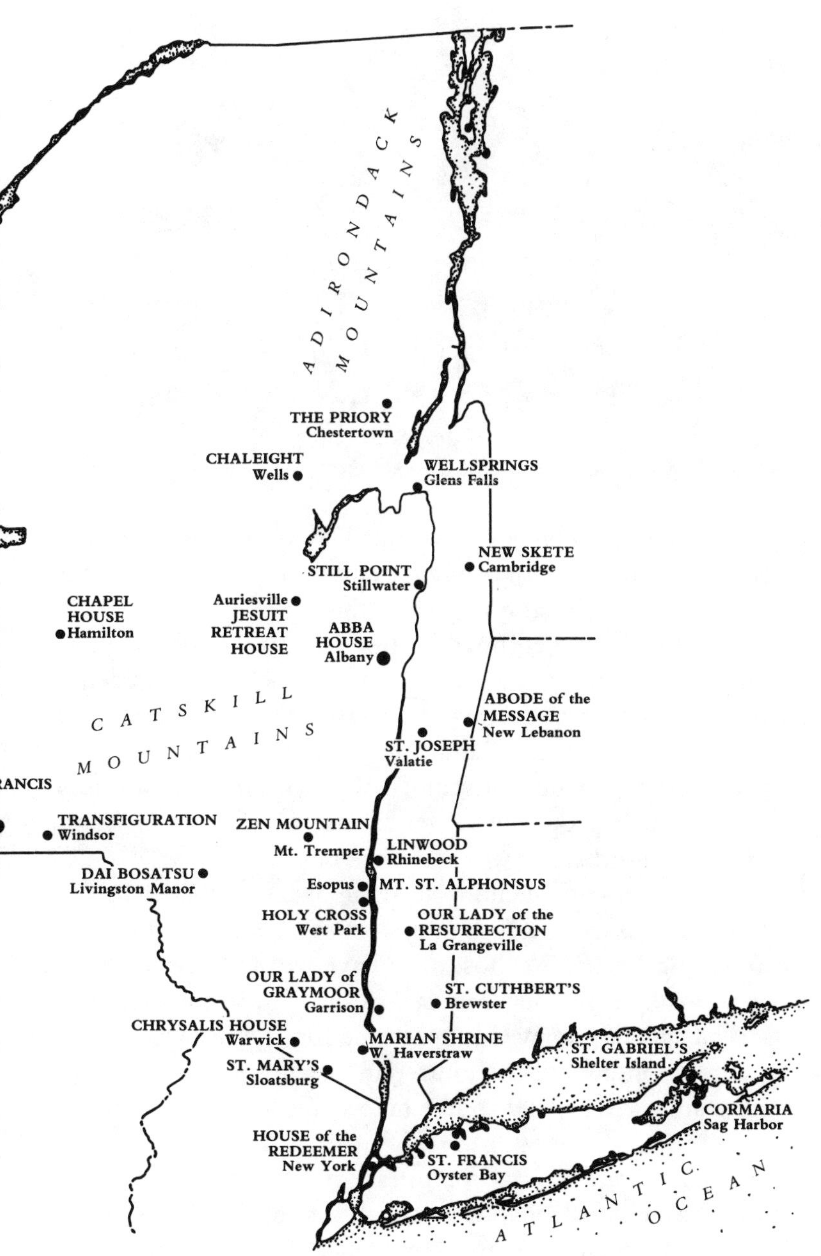
ADIRONDACK MOUNTAINS
THE PRIORY
Chestertown
CHALEIGHT
Wells
WELLSPRINGS
Glens Falls
NEW SKETE
Cambridge
STILL POINT
Stillwater
CHAPEL HOUSE
Hamilton
Auriesville
JESUIT RETREAT HOUSE
ABBA HOUSE
Albany
CATSKILL MOUNTAINS
ABODE of the MESSAGE
New Lebanon
ST. JOSEPH
Valatie
RANCIS
TRANSFIGURATION
Windsor
ZEN MOUNTAIN
Mt. Tremper
LINWOOD
Rhinebeck
DAI BOSATSU
Livingston Manor
Esopus
MT. ST. ALPHONSUS
HOLY CROSS
West Park
OUR LADY of the RESURRECTION
La Grangeville
OUR LADY of GRAYMOOR
Garrison
ST. CUTHBERT'S
Brewster
CHRYSALIS HOUSE
Warwick
MARIAN SHRINE
W. Haverstraw
ST. GABRIEL'S
Shelter Island
ST. MARY'S
Sloatsburg
CORMARIA
Sag Harbor
HOUSE of the REDEEMER
New York
ST. FRANCIS
Oyster Bay
ATLANTIC OCEAN

Abba House of Prayer
Albany, NY

In 1971, following the advice of Brother David Steindl-Rast, who said, "You must start a house of prayer and your ministry will find you," an intercongregational group of Catholic nuns formed a community house and began their house of prayer. In 1980 they acquired this substantial, charming, old-fashioned house in a residential neighborhood of Albany. Taking the name Abba (Aramaic, Hebrew, and Arabic for "father," and thus meaning God the Father), they work to develop a true community of prayer for the community at large, in which people of all faiths can join for a few hours, days, weeks, or months.

Individuals can come to spend time alone or take either a directed retreat or a spiritual sabbatical—an opportunity for rest and renewal of body, mind, and spirit for those who have worked hard and need a temporary break from their regular, heavy commitments. Abba has also served as a home away from home for a young college girl whose parents, members of the Hutterian Brethren—an Anabaptist community—arranged for her to live here while attending school in Albany.

There are 15 private rooms for guests, with shared bathrooms available in a homelike atmosphere. Breakfast and lunch are picked up in the efficient kitchen. The evening meal is taken in a relaxed atmosphere with other guests and the community in the dining room. The nuns have two daily prayer sessions in the chapel on the main floor: the first, in early afternoon, is planned so that guests have the entire morning free; the second, shorter session is held after the evening meal. The chapel is always open for prayer and meditation. Both the large enclosed yard and the neighborhood are good for walking, and guests may use nearby swimming pools.

Abba House is a center of hospitality and interaction for concerned persons of all ages and backgrounds. The classes held here are aimed at a deeper understanding of peace and justice. In a true spirit of cooperation, Abba has joined with Barry House, an Anglican retreat in Brant Lake, New York, to provide and encourage individuals and groups to become familiar with and use both prayer houses; one may be more suitable than the other, depending on size of group or time of year, but visitors are encouraged to consider either one, since, as they say, "We honor the same God."

Abba House of Prayer
647 Western Ave.
Albany, NY 12203
(518) 438-8320

Accommodations: *5 singles and doubles for men and women; pick-up breakfast and lunch, 6 P.M. communal dinner; daily community prayer; atmosphere of silence; closed in August; $20 a night.*

Directions: *From the west or south, take I-87 (New York State Thruway) to Exit 24, then take the first exit on the right to Western Ave. (Rte. 20). At the end of the road, turn left on Western Ave. toward downtown, past the State University, for about 3 miles. Abba House is on the left side of Western Ave., at the corner of Homestead Avenue. (Do not be misled by Homestead Street, on the right.) There is a traffic light at the corner. Homestead Ave. is almost opposite Euclid Ave. on the right. Park on Homestead Ave. and use the side entrance.*

From the north, take I-87 (Northway) and go past all Albany exits to the end of the road. Turn left on Western Ave., and from that point follow instructions above.

From the east, on I-90, take Exit B1 (Albany/Rte. 90). Continue on Rte. 90 past the Albany exits. Follow signs for Rte. 90/Buffalo. Take Exit 1 South (Western Ave./Rte. 20), and follow instructions above.

Abbey of the Genesee
Piffard, NY

In the early 1950s an affluent couple offered this land to the local Catholic diocese for the purpose of founding a monastery. The Cistercian order at Gethsemani, where Thomas Merton lived, sent a group of monks to Piffard to develop a monastic community. The 500 original acres were already a working farm with a main house and barns, and over the years the property has grown to approximately 2,200 acres.

The first monks modified the house to suit their communal style. They farmed the land to raise wheat, corn, and soybeans, following the Rule of St. Benedict, which demands that its followers earn their living by their own hands and make enough also to help the poor. During those early days, the cook, an ex-navy chef, made bread for the community. Visitors were so impressed with the bread's taste and quality that they wanted to take some home. So a business was started, and today the highly mechanized bakery turns out 30,000 loaves of Monk's Bread a week, on a three-day work schedule, and this is sufficient to support the community. The monks donate 1,000 loaves a week to the poor, using their own truck to deliver them to various distribution points in the Rochester area. They also make delicious fruitcakes in a variety of flavors, including an extraordinary butterscotch.

The monks lead a rigorous life that begins with prayers at 2:25 A.M.

Throughout the day, they meet to sing the canonical hours and spend about three hours in community prayer and song. Visitors are welcome at these services, which are held in the main chapel built with rocks found on the monastery land and in the Genesee River. The somber wood-and-stone interior, with its simple religious decorations and jewellike stained-glass windows, has a natural dignity, as though a cave had been modified for worship.

There are three separate guesthouses about one-half mile from the chapel. The original monastery, called Bethlehem ("house of bread"), has single rooms, former monks' cells, each with a single bed, chair, and desk, and there are communal washrooms. Meals, provided by the staff, are pick-up breakfasts of cereal and monk's bread, with hot water available for coffee or tea. The main meal at noon is usually a hearty stew or pasta with salads and vegetables and simple desserts. Supper is often just soup and salad, but snacks of peanut butter and jelly sandwiches, fruit, and hot drinks are always available. At the other guesthouses, Bethany and Cana, guests cook for themselves. Visitors can help with meal preparations and cleanup. Occasionally, men may work in the bakery.

This is, by reputation, one of the strictest Cistercian communities in the United States, and various monks are available for discussion and counseling. As one of the monks said, "This place allows people to look inside and examine the rhythms they are living by. Often those who come are in transition. This place allows them to step off the merry-go-round of today's fast world and take a look at their internal show."

Abbey of the Genesee
3258 River Rd.
Piffard, NY 14533
(716) 243-2220 (Mon., Wed., Fri., 9 A.M.–noon)

Accommodations: *3 guesthouses with 51 beds, mainly simple singles; buffet in silence with guest community, or self-cooked meals; canonical hours; 2,200 acres; work option; excellent bookstore; open year-round. Free-will donation.*

Directions: *Piffard is 35 miles south of Rochester, New York, 6 miles west of Geneseo on Rte. 63. Watch for the abbey sign on the right.*

Abode of the Message
New Lebanon, NY

Located on 430 acres in the Berkshire Mountains, on property bought from Shakers, the Sufi Order in the West has a thriving community of close to 100 adults and children. The Abode of the Message was founded in 1975 by Pir Vilayat Khan to provide a supportive environment for self-discovery.

The community follows the traditions of Sufism, in which life is seen as a garden where all possibilities exist for creativity and the expression of beauty. By continually developing, expanding, and refining one's ideals and overcoming self-imposed limitations, one gains a new perspective on life as one becomes aware that we are all one family, one body.

The community has restored the 19th-century Shaker buildings to serve the needs of the group. Families have apartments and meet in the main dining room for meals. The food is prepared by a rotating kitchen staff, and varies from gourmet vegetarian to cheese sandwiches. The atmosphere is cheerful and open, and visitors feel welcome and comfortable.

Meditation sessions are held every day in the meditation hall, a large, barnlike structure that can accommodate the entire community. There are regular evening sessions of special breathing techniques and exercises, conducted by the more experienced members. Services and classes are open to all, and are regularly attended by neighbors and guests.

Individuals and couples can come for visits of up to three days and live with the community. The rooms are simply but comfortably furnished. There are separate community washrooms for men and women. On the second floor of the main building is a large reading room with sofas, easy chairs, and good reading lights.

On a hill above the community buildings are hermitage retreats where individuals can spend from one to ten nights. These simple, one-room huts, each in a private natural setting, have commanding views of the valley below. Retreatants should bring sleeping bags and be prepared to use an outhouse. Food is available from the main kitchen. One spends time completely alone, except for a daily visit from the retreat master.

The community does not promote a particular creed or church, but works to unite the followers of different religions and faiths in wisdom. It believes a greater trust and confidence will be established among people in this way.

Abode of the Message
Box 1030D, Shaker Rd.
***New Lebanon, NY** 12125*
(518) 794-8090

Accommodations: *Men, women, and children are welcome as space is available in community housing or simple hermitages; community vegetarian meals; daily meditation; 430 acres; open year-round; $35 a day.*

Directions: *East from Albany on U.S. 20, go through New Lebanon toward Pittsfield. About 2 miles outside New Lebanon, watch for the white sign (unlit) on the right for Darrow School. Enter this small road and continue on past the school for another mile. You will see the Abode on the left, at the sign MOUNTAIN ROAD SCHOOL.*

The Chaleight
Wells, NY

The town of Wells, population 500, is on the edge of the 6-million-acre Adirondack State Park (the largest park in the United States), and the Chaleight at Griffin Gorge Commons is on the outskirts of Wells. This 40-acre retreat has five private homes and one barn with an apartment that is being modified into a health-food store and restaurant. The 11 people who live here share common views on life, health, and happiness. They are family-oriented and gather to celebrate holidays, birthdays, weddings, the equinox, and the solstices. Each summer they construct an Indian sweat lodge, where hot rocks are put in an enclosed tent and sprinkled with water. The constant high temperature causes intense sweating and both a physical and spiritual cleansing. The community cares deeply for the land and people who dwell on it, and tries to live in simple awareness of the relationship between the two and the responsibility for future generations.

The Chaleight—a chalet-style structure in the form of a figure eight—was built from materials salvaged from two razed historic buildings, an old hotel and a barn. The two-level cabin with rounded rooms sits out of sight from the road, on a high point overlooking a pond. The unusual shape allows an even dispersion of heat from the woodstove. Water comes from a gravity-fed spring, and gas lamps add charm and warmth to the wooden interior. There is no electricity or telephone. Four adults can sleep and live here comfortably.

Up on the hill behind the Chaleight are rock formations that indicate an ancient Native American burial site. This is sacred ground where, centuries ago, religious ceremonies were held by the first inhabitants of this land. Aside from a path having been cleared and leaves and fallen branches removed, the area is kept just as it was discovered some years ago. It is a beautiful, thickly wooded place, perfect for meditation and reflection.

There is an informal community meeting held weekly to assess projects and review future plans. Anyone interested in this life-style of environmental concern and appreciation is welcome to visit and spend some time.

The Chaleight
Griffin Gorge Commons
Rte. *30,* ***Box*** *341*
Wells, NY *12190*
(518) 924-2112

Accommodations: *4 or more people can be comfortably housed in this unique lodge with cooking facilities; 40 acres on the edge of a forest preserve; open year-round; $250 a weekend, $400 a week, or work exchange for camping space and/or food.*

Directions: *Take I-87 (New York State Thruway) north of Albany to Rte. 30, north to Wells, New York.*

Chapel House
Hamilton, NY

In the mid-1950s, an anonymous donation made it possible to build and endow Chapel House. The concept was to establish a place where anyone with initiative and interest could come to stay, have access to books of religious insight and recordings of liturgical music, be surrounded by sacred art, and have the time and space provided by a chapel for meditation and spiritual devotion.

The beautiful building is on a high point of the Colgate University grounds, away from the bustle of campus life and just across from the great lawns that used to serve as golf fairways. The chapel contains no religious symbols; it is simply a quiet space for prayer and contemplation. Next door is a reception room leading to the library, which holds several thousand volumes of significant books on every religion. There are comfortable reading chairs and tables for serious study. Works of art, including a Tibetan prayer mantle, grace the walls between the bookshelves, and over the stone fireplace hangs a fine Jewish sculpture of intricate brasswork. On the other side of the reception room is a music room with a high-quality sound system and a vast selection of records. The music was chosen for its religious or spiritual nature and includes not only works by Beethoven and Bach but also by those who would not generally be considered composers of sacred music. The room is decorated with

Zen calligraphy, a crucifix, a superb Buddha, and many other marvelous artifacts.

Beyond the music room is the dining room, where three meals a day are served by the resident supervisor. Downstairs are seven single rooms, each with private bath, single bed, chair, desk and more than 20 books as part of the basic furnishings. The windows look out on a quiet woodland setting.

Guests are requested to observe silence except during mealtimes. The only other requirement is that visitors use the facilities for their personal religious research and that they do not disturb the privacy of others.

The chapel has been used as a place of worship by Christians, Jews, Hindus, Buddhists, and Muslims. There is no guru or master teacher here. Visitors are expected to seek guidance in the books, music, and works of art that have been proven by time to be great teachers. The anonymous benefactor of Chapel House once said with a twinkle in her eye, "If one person a year comes and uses it for the purposes we have in mind . . . we will have a good income from our investment."

Chapel House
Colgate University
***Hamilton, NY** 13346*
*(315) 824-1000, **ext.** 675*

Accommodations: *7 private rooms with bath for men and women; meals served in guest dining room; chapel; silence strictly observed, except at meals; extensive religious book, music, and art collection; guests are requested to stay a minimum of 2 nights and are asked to confine themselves to Chapel House property above the campus during their stay; open year-round; $15 a night suggested.*

Directions: *From I-87 (New York State Thruway), take Exit 24 (Northway). Proceed west on Rte. 20. At Madison, turn south on 12B to Hamilton. Once on Colgate campus, go uphill, bearing to the right, to reach Chapel House.*

Chautauqua Institution

Chautauqua, NY

In 1874 a summer school was held on the shores of Lake Chautauqua to instruct Sunday-school teachers in organization, management, and teaching methods. From this modest beginning the programs were expanded to include political concepts, economics, literature, science, and music study. Hotels and rooming houses were built to house the ever-increasing numbers of visitors. By the early 1900s a grand hotel was built, and the summer-camp concept of a few weeks in a tent made a transition to a more genteel approach to education, which included clean sheets and an elegant dining room. Business leaders of the day, such as Henry Ford, attended, and Thomas Edison and his family came regularly.

Many religious groups either built or acquired good-sized houses and created as many rooms as possible, which they made—and still make—available for rent, with community kitchen facilities. Before the end of the 19th century, Chautauqua had become a national force as a way to reach thousands of people interested in personal growth through education. Here, in one place, grew a culture camp on the shores of a clean, clear lake where one could swim, boat, fish, and be entertained by nightly concerts and lectures from prominent speakers.

By the early 20th century, many more private homes were built on the grounds, and the 210-acre setting became a typical small town of the era. And it remains so today: an almost classic community in a sylvan setting; beautifully kept, Victorian-style houses with lush green lawns and clipped hedges, large porches with comfortable sitting arrangements, flowers growing along walkways. Many of the houses have gingerbread decorations, are painted in light pastel shades, and are in good condition and well maintained. Auto access is limited, so one can walk the streets or ride a bicycle and slow the pace of physical movement to allow the mind to rest and wonder.

The Chautauqua Program runs for nine weeks, from mid-June to the end of August. After Labor Day, things are really quiet, but there are more than 200 regular residents who stay year-round, and many of the rooming houses and some hotels are available. The fine library on Bestor Plaza remains open, as do the post office and newsstand/book-and-gift shop.

This community is a piece of Americana, an outdoor museum of late 19th- and early 20th-century life-style. One can wander for hours admiring the fine houses, look out to the lake that is never far away, sit on the well-situated benches, and be undisturbed for hours or days at a time. A perfect place to read, relax, ruminate, and get one's internal wheels balanced.

Chautauqua Institution
***P.O. Box** 1095*
***Chautauqua, NY** 14722*
(716) 357-6200

Accommodations: *For men, women, and children, a wide range of accommodations in summer, from the grand Athenaeum Hotel ([716] 357-4444) to rooming houses and church guesthouses. (Chautauqua Accommodations Referral Service, Chautauqua, NY 14722, phone [716] 357-6204, is open year-round).*

Directions: *South of Buffalo, and near Jamestown, New York, the Chautauqua Institution is easily accessible via I-90. Take Exit 60 (Westfield) and follow Rte. 394 East to Mayville and along the lake to the entrance.*

Chrysalis House

Warwick, NY

The community of laypeople who live in this large, modern house surrounded by 10 landscaped acres operates as a center for contemplative living under the guidance of Father Thomas Keating, a Trappist monk. It is affiliated with the Archdiocese of New York.

In the early 1980s, Father Keating invited a number of people to the Lama Foundation in New Mexico, where he gave a 16-day retreat on contemplative living and centering prayer. This was the first time he had done this, and his purpose was to encourage formation of a network of lay communities affiliated with a local diocese, the focus of each being service, centering prayer, and contemplative living. Keating planned to serve as spiritual adviser, and meet with these people three or four times a year.

Like the butterfly pupa, which is encased in a chrysalis while it rests and grows wings and a new body, Chrysalis House is a place of transformation where the false self may gradually be shed and a new person in Christ formed.

The course titled "Practices in Contemplative Living" meets one weekend a month for nine months. Building on the work done here, in and with the community, individuals continue to put the same principles into practice in their daily lives in the intervening periods. Visitors may attend for a day, overnight, or one of the regularly scheduled retreats.

There is a monastic-type schedule beginning at the 5 A.M. wake-up bell, followed by 5:30 morning prayer, mass at a local church, then solitude for prayer, and a pick-up breakfast before the 9 A.M.-to-noon work period. Midday prayer is followed by the main meal with the community, at which conversation is permitted. At 2 P.M. there is work or recreation until 5:30 evening prayer. Silence is observed from the conclusion of evening prayer until 9 A.M. the next day.

Members of the original assemblage of prayer group leaders and others founded this house as a functioning contemplative community, recognizing that spiritual growth is a continuous process of prayer, solitude, and silence.

This remarkable place is obviously meeting a real need, for in 1986 there were 1,200 names on the mailing list, and by the end of 1989 there were more than 12,000.

Note: As this book was going to press, Chrysalis House moved to larger premises, so although all the details of accommodations and directions apply to the new location, the drawing is of the building visited in 1990 (also in Warwick).

Chrysalis House
235 Lake-Bellvale Rd.
Warwick, NY 10990
(914) 986-8050

Accommodations: *For men and women, 22 beds in singles and doubles; vegetarian food; 10 acres of landscaped grounds; contemplative community; open year-round; suggested offering: $25 a night.*

Directions: *From I-87 (New York State Thruway), take Exit 15. Follow Rte. 17 North 9 miles. Turn left on Rte. 17A, through Greenwood Lake. Follow Rte. 17A West 10 miles. In the hamlet of Bellvale turn right on Iron Forge Rd. and continue 2.3 miles (Iron Forge Rd. becomes Lake-Bellvale Rd.). Chrysalis House is set back from the road on the left.*

New Jersey Transit has express service to Warwick from the New York Port Authority Terminal ([212] 564-8484). You will be met in Warwick at the Bellvale bus stop.

Cormaria Center
St. Mark's House of Prayer
Sag Harbor, NY

Set on 17 acres fronting Northwest Bay is the Catholic retreat house called Cormaria. The main section was built in the early 1900s by a sea captain for his private residence. The story goes that the captain got his ship's carpenter to do the fine interior woodwork, and it is splendid. There is elegant Tiffany glass around the dining-room ceiling and windows, which command a spectacular, uninterrupted view of the bay.

Off the main entrance is the chapel, decorated in a nautical motif. A back corner is hung with fishing nets and shells placed on the wall; boat oars separate the altar from the pews. The windows offer a glimpse of the sea. To the other side of the entrance foyer is the large dining room, a section added to the original house, where home-cooked meals are served cafeteria-style. There is a residence wing for up to 75 persons in clean, comfortable single rooms with community washrooms. Meeting and crafts rooms are on the lower level.

The nuns of the Religious of the Sacred Heart of Mary see hospitality to a large variety of guests as a natural part of their mission. Their regular retreat programs cover every need, including continuous spiritual direction.

At the edge of the property is a small building that has two separate hermitages for those who prefer to spend their time alone.

Another separate, small, shingled house, St. Mark's House of Prayer, provides accommodations for two to five people. This self-contained prayer house, cozy and homey, has five prayer sessions daily from 6:20 A.M. to 8 P.M., which guests may attend.

Cormaria, in its tranquil setting, offers a variety of opportunities for spiritual sustenance and rebirth. One retreatant, a Brahmin, wrote a thank-you note to the director in which he said, "The peace that I found hasn't left me."

Cormaria Center
St. Mark's House of Prayer
Bay St.
***Sag Harbor, NY** 11963*
(516) 725-4206 ***(Cormaria)***
(516) 725-3365 ***(St. Mark's)***

Accommodations: *Cormaria can house 30–35 men and women in singles, or 80 in doubles; there is also a hermitage; St. Mark's has room for 3–5; daily prayers; 17 bayfront acres and quiet lanes of Sag Harbor for walking; open year-round except over Christmas holidays; $35 a day at Cormaria; free-will offering at St. Mark's.*

Directions: *From the Long Island Expressway, take Exit 70. Turn right off the exit ramp and continue to the end of the road, and continue east on Rte. 27 (following the Montauk signs) into Bridgehampton. Turn left at the Bridgehampton monument onto the Sag Harbor Turnpike, and proceed about 4 miles into Sag Harbor, continuing through the village to the foot of Main St. (windmill). Turn right onto Bay St.; 3,000 feet past the yacht basin and the oil tanks, the sign indicating Cormaria is on the left.*

Dai Bosatsu Zendo
Livingston Manor, NY

The approach to the zendo winds along a narrow road for twenty miles, and by the time one reaches it, it is as though one has passed through a time warp and come upon a place deep in the mountains of Japan; only there, it seems, could one find such a magnificent temple. The monastery is at the edge of Beecher Lake, the highest lake in the Catskill Mountains, which the naturalist John Burroughs described in 1868: "As beautiful as a dream . . . the mind is delighted as an escaped bird, and darts gleefully from point to point." The 30-acre lake has changed little since then, or even since the time it was revered by the Leni-Lenape Indians, who believed that the mountain waters restored vitality to both mind and body. The monastery was completed in 1976, and since then has offered students the opportunity for intensive training in a traditional Zen monastery environment. As authentic inside as out, the quality of its construction is evident from the gleaming oak floors to the windows that act as picture frames for the forest, the lake, and the abundant wildlife.

As part of the Zen Studies Society established to aid D. T. Suzuki in his efforts to introduce Zen Buddhism to the West, this zendo, only three hours from New York City, has a full schedule of retreats ranging from weekends to full weeks. Anyone is welcome to visit the monastery or guesthouses and to join in the daily sitting sessions in the meditation room. In twice-weekly classes, the 17 monks and students in residence ponder how to become a stronger and more compassionate Buddhist community. One way has been to invite outside groups, such as AA, to come to meetings. Those held in 1988 were so successful that the program doubled in size in 1989. Participants who came with no knowledge or experience of Zen training have returned again and again, and many now sit regularly.

As a result of reaching out to this and other groups, the monks have become less isolated, and the awareness of Zen practice is growing in the world. As one monk wrote, "Real Zen practice opens out. It is wisdom and compassion in action. . . . If compassion in action is present in society, it will become clearly evident in the actions of that society."

In addition to the monastery and the 14-room lakeside guesthouse, there is also a cottage for as many as ten (dormitory style) or just a few. This building has a solarium with hanging plants and flowers.

Dai Bosatsu Zendo
HCR 1, Box 171
Livingston Manor, NY 12758
(914) 439-4566 (8 A.M.–noon)

Accommodations: *Monastery comfortably houses 75 men and women in singles and doubles; guesthouse holds 20; meals are vegetarian and taken in silence at the monastery; separate kitchen at the guesthouse; optional zazen with the community; work requirement for those staying at the monastery; 2,000-volume library; yoga; lake, hiking on 1,400 acres; open year-round; suggested donation: $50 a night.*

Directions: *From New York City, follow Palisades Pkwy. to Rte. 6, to Rte. 17 West. From Rte. 17 West, take Exit 96 (Livingston Manor), and go right under Rte. 17. At the stop sign, turn right toward Lew Beach. Turn right again just past King's Katering, on Beaverkill Rd. Proceed 11 miles (through Lew Beach, past Mobil gas station, bridge) with no turns. Bear right at the Ranger Station and go straight over the bridge, past Turnwood. Follow the winding dirt road 1 mile past the white chateau, on the right. Turn left into the entrance gate, and continue 2 miles.*

Holy Cross Monastery

West Park, NY

From the entrance plaque, which reads *Crux est mundi medicina* ("The Cross is the healing of the world"), to the request that guests offer a prayer for the person who will next occupy their room, this monastery reaches out to offer solace and comfort to all who come here.

Holy Cross Monastery is an Episcopalian community of monks who follow the Benedictine traditions of monasticism. The monastery is perched on 26 acres bordering the Hudson River. The original building, a large, rambling brick mansion, was completed in 1904, and there have been additions and modifications over the years. The refectory is of superb design, with seven large arched windows looking out to meadows and woods with the river beyond, an ever-changing art gallery of the Hudson River School, painted daily by nature.

The guest rooms are generous by monastic standards, and can be reached by elevator. They are clean, neat, and comfortable, many with a river view. The monks observe a daily schedule of community prayer in the chapel beginning at 6 A.M., with the last prayer service at 7:30 P.M. The Great Silence, a lovely tradition, begins at 9 P.M. and is observed until 8:15 the next morning.

There is a regular series of retreats that explore subjects such as the spiritual dimensions of writing and art, and examine the Benedictine monastic experience, which emphasizes a balanced life of work, prayer, and relaxation. Another program focuses on healing and reaching out to those in recovery.

There is an ongoing artist-in-residence program in which serious, accomplished artists are given room and board and a place to work, based on their talent and need.

Below the chapel is the crypt where the founder of the community is interred. There is a magnificent folk-art icon donated by two artists, free spirits who had borrowed the car of an Episcopal priest in Michigan, and were grounded nearby. Rather than returning to the Midwest to explain their lengthy absence and the condition of the vehicle, which they had crashed into a tree, the artists agreed to take refuge at Holy Cross and donate their artistic talents, which were considerable, to making icons for all of the monasteries in the order. This one depicts Father James Huntington, the founder of the Order of the Holy Cross, with scenes of New York City, where the order began.

In any season, this is a lovely place to be. From the solitary walks along the river to the many quiet nooks inside, where one can read quietly, the monks maintain a warm and inviting hospitality.

Holy Cross Monastery
Box 99, Rte. 9W
***West Park, NY** 12493*
(914) 384-6660

Accommodations: *For men and women, 39 rooms including 7 doubles; delicious, homemade communal meals and snacks served in a beautiful dining room overlooking the Hudson River; canonical hours; Elderhostels; walking trails through meadows and along the river; nice bookstore; "Great Silence" 9 P.M.–8:15 A.M.; closed Mondays and month of August; suggested donation: $42.50 a night.*

Directions: *From I-87 (New York State Thruway), take Exit 18 (New Paltz). From the exit, turn right onto Rte. 299 East; take Rte. 299 to the end, where it meets Rte. 9W. Take Rte. 9W North about 4 miles into the village of West Park. The monastery is in the center of the village on the river side (right) of the road. Large signs are visible at the entrance to the drive.*

Holy Trinity Community

Hornell, NY

During July 1989, this religious lay community celebrated its first anniversary in the newly built monastery building that looks out over the hills and valleys around Hornell. The 70-acre property was purchased in the late 1970s by two Long Island couples who shared a dream of establishing a monastic community together, following the Rule of St. Benedict.

The community members, now one couple and a widow, have their separate living quarters. A large section of the monastery contains the chapel, library, lounge, kitchen, dining room, and guest rooms. The place is furnished simply, and everything about it reflects its newness.

Four times a day, everyone meets for prayer in the chapel. Visitors are welcome for a few hours of reflective quiet, or a stay of one or more nights. In keeping with the Benedictine monastic tradition, visitors are received graciously. "We get as much from our guests as they do from us," one member said.

Holy Trinity reaches out in many ways. It plans days of prayer and invites the local community to join in, using parish church bulletins to announce these meetings. It is committed to serving the outside world in whatever ways it can, such as visiting shut-ins, planning a liturgy for a conference for divorced, separated, and widowed persons, providing renewal talks for married couples, working with the hospice program and Amnesty International, and tutoring children. But the major focus is the monastic life and keeping a balanced approach to all activities.

This is very different from grand, tradition-bound monasteries. The house, with its clean lines and fresh, comfortable, but spare rooms, reflects the emerging lay commitment to religious and church evolution. The noted Catholic thinker Father Eugene Walsh, who was an ecumenical pioneer and a driving force behind the reforms of Vatican II, once wrote that "a parish does not exist to serve the needs of those who belong to the parish. The people are the parish. They exist to serve the needs of each other, and even more so, to serve the needs of those outside."

Holy Trinity Community
7200 Tobes Hill Rd.
Hornell, NY 14843
(607) 324-7624

Accommodations: *For men and women, 2 singles and one double; dining with community; prayer 4 times daily; tape and book library; 70 acres; open year-round; free-will offering.*

Directions: *Located in western New York State, in the town of Hornell. Take Main St. in Hornell to the East Main St. Bridge. Cross the bridge and immediately take Tobes Hill Rd., the uphill road to the left. Follow Tobes Hill Rd. for 1 1/2 miles until it makes a sharp right. The Holy Trinity driveway is on the left at that turn.*

House of the Redeemer

New York, NY

A few steps from Fifth Avenue and Central Park, this East Side town house was donated to the Episcopal Church of New York in 1949 by a great-granddaughter of Cornelius Vanderbilt. The five-story red brick building, with a limestone palazzo-style façade, was designed by the architect Grosvenor Atterbury and completed in 1916. Its rooms are filled with Italianate detail: carved mantels, coffered ceilings, and tiled floors, and are furnished with Baroque and Renaissance furniture. The main staircase leads to the second-floor library, a two-storied, balconied room that contains 15th-century woodwork taken from the Ducal Palace in Urbino, Italy. The ceiling medallion depicting the Urbino ducal coat of arms is attributed to Raphael, who was the court painter during this period. At one end of the room is a handsome fireplace; at the other stands a grand piano. There is an Aeolian organ built into the wall. The entire house was designed around this great room, which now serves for meetings, chamber music and solo concerts, and receptions.

Daily prayer services, morning and evening, take place in the chapel, a former drawing room on the second floor, but apart from these, there is no formal schedule.

This house provides a desperately needed facility in New York City. The Episcopal Church Center uses some of the rooms for visitors on church business, more than half of whom come from abroad. Small groups and individuals can be accommodated.

The warden writes in a recent newsletter, "A retreat is not a training, an educational, or even a religious effort. No effort whatever should be involved. It is purely spiritual, silent, powerful. We are filled with His Presence; His word speaks to us; His grace is sufficient. Be still and know that I am God!"

House of the Redeemer
7 East 95th St.
New York, NY 10028
(212) 289-0399

Accommodations: *Houses 15 men and women, with meals available; daily offices and Eucharist; large religious library and art collection; closed July and August until after expansion; $35 a night, plus $4 breakfast, $7 lunch, $12 dinner.*

Directions: *Just off Fifth Ave., convenient to buses, subways, and taxis.*

Jesuit Retreat House

Auriesville, NY

The Jesuit Retreat House is located on the grounds of the Shrine of Our Lady of Martyrs, where, more than 350 years ago, three Jesuit missionaries were killed by American Indians. The house was built in 1938 for third-year seminary students, and then in 1968 it became a retreat house for clergy and laymen. It is a fitting place for a Jesuit retreat house. Early in the 1600s, the first Black Robes—as they were known from the color of their cassocks—came into this region from Canada and set up missions among the Indian tribes. The Jesuit presence is closely linked to the history of the early European settlements throughout what was to become New York State, as the French, Dutch, and English merchants vied for the Indian furs and land, and the priests vied for their souls.

In 1884 an eminent Catholic historian identified the place where the martyrs were slain, and the Catholic Church purchased the land. The initial ceremonies were held on the Feast of the Assumption, August 15, 1885, and by the late 1890s thousands of pilgrims journeyed here every year. Buildings and more land were added, and today, during the season from early May to late October, more than 250,000 visitors come annually.

The retreat house operates year-round, and group retreats are available during the spring and fall. Private retreatants can usually be accommodated at any time. There is a classic Jesuit chapel with one large altar commemorating the martyrs; along the walls on two levels of the chapel are small altars where masses used to be said simultaneously in the days when many priests lived here.

There are about 50 single rooms, spartan but clean and efficient, with bed, desk, chair, and closet. A large dining room has a section for those maintaining silence and is open at all times for coffee, tea, and snacks. The library and reading rooms are comfortable and well stocked.

The grounds comprise more than 600 acres on a hilltop with lovely views to the east and north. There are miles of open walkways around the well-tended property, and there is an abundance of birds. A few years ago, the Sassafras Bird Club spotted 39 species on one fine day.

Jesuit Retreat House
Auriesville, NY *12016*
(518) 829-7010
(518) 853-3033

Accommodations: *For men and women, 48–50 rooms available; meals included; daily mass, 4 chapels; 600 acres; famous shrine; open May–October for retreats (church, shrine, and grounds are open longer); suggested donation: $30 a night, clergy $25.*

Directions: *From the east on I-90, take Exit 27 (Amsterdam); from the west on I-90, take Exit 28 (Fultonville). Follow signs on Rte. 5S for Auriesville. The entrance to the shrine and retreat house is well marked at the junction of Rte. 5S and Noeltner Rd.*

Linwood Spiritual Center
Rhinebeck, NY

High on a hill overlooking the Hudson River, this 65-acre property commands views to the south and west. Donated to the Sisters of St. Ursula in 1964 by Jacob Ruppert Schalk, it serves as a residence for 13 nuns, as well as a center for spiritual renewal for men and women seeking a quiet, restful place to spend a few hours or days of reflection.

Initially the nuns used the house as it was, but found the rooms either too big or too small. To solve this problem, they had it professionally burned down. Then, in 1967, they erected the present house, which has single and double rooms for twenty, two large conference rooms, a library, and a spacious chapel where mass is usually said daily. There are three dining rooms of various sizes where guests can eat together, join the community, or eat separately in silence.

There is a full schedule of retreat programs of varying lengths, organized and presented by a staff of four Ursulan nuns. The programs deal with spiritual development, a full Enneagram series based on Sufi teachings for self understanding, and ongoing weekends for twelve-step spirituality.

Saint Ursula is the patron saint of education, and the order's main thrust is still education. The first Ursulan nuns came to the United

States in the early 1900s, when the French government suppressed religious education.

The spacious grounds include a separate guesthouse, suitable for small groups, with its own kitchen and living room; a private cottage that can be used by individuals or couples as a hermitage; and a large, open pavilion with electricity, restrooms, and a fireplace where groups can gather outside in good weather.

Just a short distance from the village of Rhinebeck, this complex offers seclusion and quiet. The hospitality of the nuns who work to provide a homey atmosphere is complemented by the peaceful views of the Hudson River.

Linwood Spiritual Center
139 South Mill Rd.
***Rhinebeck, NY** 12572*
(914) 876-4178

Accommodations: *Men, women, and children are housed in the main building, which has 18 singles with sinks; the guesthouse has 9 singles and 1 double, and there is a hermitage; informal buffet meals in community or retreatant dining room; walks, tennis, swimming on 65 acres overlooking the Hudson River; open year-round; $35 a night.*

Directions: *From I-87 (New York State Thruway), take Exit 19 (Kingston). At the traffic circle, follow signs for Rte. 209 (Kingston/Rhinecliff Bridge). After crossing the Rhinecliff Bridge, proceed to the second intersection; turn right onto Rte. 9G South. At the next traffic light, turn right onto Rte. 9 South. In Rhinebeck, after passing the Beekman Arms Hotel, take the first right turn onto Mill Rd. (There is a cemetery on the corner.) Linwood is 3.3 miles on the right.*

Marian Shrine
West Haverstraw, NY

Just 30 minutes north of the George Washington Bridge is the Marian Shrine, 200 acres of pristine woodlands that look west and north to the widest part of the Hudson River. This beautiful property was acquired in 1945 by the Roman Catholic Salesian Order, founded by Saint John Bosco, patron saint of youth.

The drive looks across large expanses of lawn that slope gently up to the outdoor shrines where thousands of people come on weekends to celebrate mass. The mansion is used by the priests and brothers as a residence, and beyond the cafeteria and gift shop, the woods begin. Paths are cleared through the trees and bushes, and very modern Stations of the Cross are near the building complex. Down another path, past a Fatima shrine, a Lourdes grotto, and a re-creation of the house in which Saint John Bosco was born, is the striking entrance to the mile-long Rosary Way. The 15 mysteries of the rosary are divided into three sections: Joyful, Sorrowful, and Glorious. Each mystery is depicted by a life-size sculpture group in its own woodland setting. These sculptures are magnificent, and they happen to be here by an unusual circumstance. In the 1950s a Salesian priest, Father Giovanni, went to Carrara, Italy, to order two statues of Saint John Bosco from the sculptor and statuemaker Enrico Arrighini. After Father Giovanni had placed his order, Arrighini invited him out to the back of his studio and showed him the 15 mystery groupings, which had been commissioned by someone who had now died. Arrighini offered to sell them for only $1,000 each. It was reported that Father Giovanni said yes faster than any Salesian before or since.

The artist Martin Luman Winter, who executed the modern sculpted Stations of the Cross, also did the giant Madonna statue, which is 48 feet tall. This was cast in Pistoia, Italy, in 1959 and eventually placed here, on a star-shaped pedestal of Vermont stone, in 1977.

Tucked behind the main building and connected to it by a walkway is a tastefully designed motel-like structure that has 50 double rooms. The rooms are connected by a labyrinth of corridors that lead to a library and indoor chapel and upstairs to a dining room, where meals are taken buffet-style. Along the corridor is a sitting room where coffee and tea are available at all hours. There is a separate building for youth retreats and, at the eastern end of the property, fields for baseball and soccer.

Formal retreats of varying length are offered, and private retreatants are also accommodated. This is a lovely, friendly place to spend time.

Marian Shrine
Filors Lane
West Haverstraw, NY *10993*
(914) 947-2200

Accommodations: *For men, women, and children, 50 modern rooms with double beds and bath; 9-room cottage; 100-bed dorm for youth groups; cafeteria; 200 acres; open year-round; $28 a night.*

Directions: *Just 30 minutes north of the George Washington Bridge. From Palisades Parkway take Exit 14 and follow Rte. 9W to the first intersection in Stony Point, then drive west on Filors Lane to the entrance.*

Mount Irenaeus Franciscan Mountain Retreat

West Clarksville, NY

This mountain retreat, named after a revered Franciscan friar, is a 228-acre farm high in the Allegheny Mountains, with views to the south and east over the magnificently wooded western edges of the Appalachian Range. The main house, which has a large living room with fireplace and adjoining dining room and porch, is a gathering space for meals. The three cabins, off in the woods a respectable distance from the main house and from each other, have kitchens where visitors can cook and fend for themselves. Self-sufficiency in the context of community is encouraged at Mt. Irenaeus, and pitching a tent is also possible, if visitors are so inclined.

The chapel was framed in one weekend by a loyal group of people who wanted to contribute their energy by helping to build a communal house of worship. The lovely structure was raised in a nondenominational spirit for the enjoyment of people of all religious persuasions. Set apart from the main house and cabins, on one of the highest spots on the farm, it looks down over the hills and valley.

The altar is in the center of the chapel; low steps lead down to it. Window seats are built beneath the large, clear windows that frame the vistas beyond. Pillows are scattered about, as though someone's comfortable home were temporarily being used as a place of worship. The lower level of the chapel is a library where one may choose a book to read.

Many of the programs are inspired by the thoughts and actions of Saint Francis of Assisi, who, with his early followers, went to the woods and mountains to seek a clearer vision of life. There are also evenings of prayer and reflection from the writings of Thomas Merton, who taught at St. Bonaventure University before becoming a Trappist.

There is much to be done at this young retreat haven, and help is always appreciated, whether it is weeding the garden, clearing brush, helping to cook or clean, chopping wood, or maintaining the hiking trails. Yet none of this is required. The earnest hope of Mt. Irenaeus is that people will come to enjoy the serenity and peace that is there, and thus find it within themselves.

Mount Irenaeus Franciscan Mountain Retreat
West Clarksville, NY
Mailing address:
St. Bonaventure University
St. Bonaventure, NY *14778*
(716) 973-2470

Accommodations: *For men, women, and children. A farmhouse for 8 with community meals, many made with vegetables and fruit from their own garden, plus a 2-bedroom cabin and 2 hermitages with kitchens; daily mass, morning and evening prayer; potluck brunch following Sunday liturgy; 228 mountaintop acres for hiking, camping, working; open year-round; suggested donation: $15 a night.*

Directions: *Located in western New York State near West Clarksville, 1 1/2 hours southwest of Buffalo. From the northwest or west, take Rte. 17 (Southern Tier Expressway) to Exit 28 (Cuba). Go south on Rte. 305 to County Rte. 1. Turn left and drive 3–4 miles. Take the second unpaved road to the right (look for the Mt. Irenaeus sign). Bear right. Turn right at Robert's Rd. (sign is on the left). Go to the top of the hill on the left.*

From the southeast or southwest, take Rte. 417 to Portville, New York. At Portville, take Rte. 305 North. Just past West Clarksville, turn right at County Rte. 1 and take the second unpaved road to the right as above.

Mount St. Alphonsus Spiritcare Center

Esopus, NY

This enormous building sits in a pristine setting on a knoll overlooking the Hudson River, with more than 400 acres of land. Just inside the main building entrance is the Romanesque chapel, an outstanding example of Byzantine influence in decoration and design. It's worth a visit just to see how splendid it is.

In 1904 the Catholic Redemptorist Fathers bought this riverfront land as a site for their new House of Studies. It took three years to complete the building, which resembles the English Houses of Parliament. From 1907 to 1985 it served as a seminary for training missionary priests, and 80 percent of the graduates were sent to foreign missions. In 1987 the mission of Mount St. Alphonsus was redirected to retreat work. There is a full spectrum of programs including prayer days and retreat weekends that offer spiritual sustenance to youths and senior groups, religious and laypeople, Protestants and Orthodox, and AA groups.

The generous design of the building, with wide corridors and high ceilings throughout, is reflected in the spacious, comfortable guest rooms, many with a river view. The dining room on the lower level is equipped to handle large groups; the food is carefully prepared by a professional staff. There are large conference rooms and smaller meeting rooms to accommodate groups of varying sizes.

The outstanding library contains more than 100,000 volumes of books on theology, psychology, the humanities, and sociology. There are also more than 2,000 periodicals. The library is a research source of great value to clergy and graduate-level students. The galleried bookshelves have hideaways and windows to sit by and read without interruption. The grounds of the property are open and well tended, complemented by miles of hiking trails along the river.

In a nearby convent there is a community of Redemptoristines, a contemplative order of nuns who have a few guest rooms available. The nuns are wholly oriented to a life of prayer, and come together six times a day to pray in their own chapel. Guests are welcome.

Mount St. Alphonsus Spiritcare Center
Rte. 9W
***Esopus, NY** 12429*
(914) 384-6550 ***(Mount St. Alphonsus)***
(914) 384-6583 ***(Redemptoristines)***

Accommodations: *For men and women, 116 beds in singles and doubles; chef from Culinary Institute of America; fabulous chapel; 400 acres with one mile of riverfront; 6–7 miles of walking trails; 100,000-volume religious library; mass and evening prayer; open year-round; $42 a night. (Our Mother of Perpetual Help, Redemptoristine Nuns have 2 double rooms available in a simple, contemplative monastery on the property.)*

Directions: *From I-87 (New York State Thruway), take Exit 17 (New Paltz), or 18 (Kingston). Drive south from Kingston on Rte. 32, into Rte. 9W, through Port Ewen, to Esopus. Drive north from New Paltz by going right at the Thruway exit onto Rte. 299 East, and left at the T onto Rte. 9W North.*

Mount St. Francis Hermitage
Maine, NY

In 1974, Father Stephen Valenta, a Franciscan for 45 years and an ordained Catholic priest for 38 years, came back to central New York State after a sabbatical year in Italy, and arranged to acquire more than 50 acres of hilltop land. Having spent a good deal of his ministry as a marriage counselor and chaplain to students at SUNY-Binghamton, he felt the time had come "to be more holy." Following the example of Jesus, he was "going to the mountain to be with my Father." He hoped that in quiet and solitude he would hear God's message more clearly and then be able to share it with others.

Since those first months, when Father Valenta lived in a tent, he has built a chapel, a conference center, and eight small hermitage cabins in the woods. As he says, "The soul becomes swollen when it hurts, so the remedy is get away from the cause of the swelling. The purpose of Mount St. Francis is as an oasis of the spirit. Usually we push so hard we can't calm down long enough to be human. People need a place where they can take a break, where they can see their lives in perspective." He himself is now on sabbatical.

Retreatants bring their own food and are left alone in their own cabins with a single bed, desk, and chair, small kitchenette, and toilet facilities. Individuals are expected to structure their own time. Mass is said daily in the chapel, and all are welcome.

There are two ponds to stroll around, and down another wooded path are outdoor Stations of the Cross. The views are lovely to the west across the mountains.

There is always some maintenance work for those who are so inclined: raking leaves, clearing paths, cutting wood, tending the garden, or whatever task can use an extra hand. But the main reason to come here is to stop the doing and simply *be*—to be trusting, loving, and grateful, and discover the depth of soul where those things originate.

Mount St. Francis Hermitage
P.O. Box 276
Maine, NY 13802
(607) 754-9813

Accommodations: *For men and women, 8 single cabins (prayer shelters) with electricity. Retreatants provide their own food and bedding; shower and indoor plumbing in main building; 200 acres with ponds; work available; closed January; suggested donation: $8 a night.*

Directions: *From Binghamton, drive West on Rte. 17. Take exit 67, and follow Rte. 26 North, through town, for five or six miles to Union Center. Once within the town, take first right, Nanticoke Dr., crossing the bridge and immediately turning left onto Edson Rd. Drive about 1 mile and take the first right, through the wrought-iron gate and up the hill into the parking area.*

Mount Saviour Monastery

Pine City, NY

The tree-lined road to Mount Saviour winds through long, rolling green fields, dotted with grazing sheep, almost as if an artist had painted them there to add color and poignancy. The Catholic Benedictine monks first came to the top of this mountain, near Elmira, in 1951. They acquired an abandoned farm, and now hold close to 1,000 acres, about 250 of which are cleared and fenced to maintain 600 sheep. To keep the monastery self-sufficient, the wool is sold as yarn, rugs, and sleeping pads. The spring shearing is an exciting time, when the monks round up the balky flock to relieve them of their winter coats.

The monastery complex is built around an octagonal chapel whose tall spire rises above the central altar. The monks sing the canonical hours here, and guests are welcome at all services. A bell is rung to call all to worship, and the monks file in, wearing gray cowled habits. The liturgy sung by these devout men is a moving and holy experience. At the conclusion of Compline, the last service of the day, the monks descend to the crypt, guests following, to sing the final prayer around the candlelit 14th-century statue of Our Lady, Queen of Peace.

Single men stay in St. Joseph's, which was the first monastery building. Each room has a cot, a desk, a chair, and a small closet. The common washroom is at the end of the corridor. On the lower level is a library and a large living room with chairs grouped or set singly by windows that look onto the lawns and pastures. Coffee and tea can be made in the kitchen, and meals are taken with the monks in the new monastery nearby.

Women and couples stay at St. Gertrude's, a refurbished farmhouse 15 minutes' walk up the road from the chapel. This charming house has clean, fresh rooms, watercolors of monastery scenes hung on the walls, and homelike furnishings. Meals are served family-style in a glass-enclosed porch.

Guests are expected to structure their own time in a way that suits their need for quiet and reflection. There are many places on the property, indoors and out, to find solitude. One can wander into the fields and in the evening look down to the Elmira Airport and watch the lights of the far-off planes, or sit on lawn chairs, looking to the south, and see the glow from the villages in the valley below. The chapel is open all day, and in the crypt there are several altars, with one section set apart for the Blessed Sacrament. This room, with benches and carpet, is a perfect place for meditation.

Mount Saviour Monastery
1825 Mount Saviour Rd.
Pine City, NY 14871
(607) 734-1688 (10–10:30 A.M.; 5–5:30 P.M.)

Accommodations: *For men, women, and children, St. Gertrude's farmhouse has 3 doubles and 3 singles; St. Peter's can house 4 people, and 2 private cottages have 2 beds each, and kitchens; 15 men's singles in the original monastery; community meals; work opportunities on the farm; beautiful gift and book shop; open all year for stays of 2 nights or more; suggested donation: $20 a night.*

Directions: *The monastery is just south of Elmira. From the east, on Rte. 17, take the second Elmira exit (Church St./Rte. 352). Follow Church St. through the city to Rte. 225. Turn left on Rte. 225, and proceed 4 miles to Mount Saviour Rd.*

From the west, Rte. 17 passes through Corning. Just past Corning Hospital, at the last traffic light in town, turn right onto Rte. 225 and bear left. Proceed about 10–11 miles on Rte. 225 until you see the Mount Saviour sign on your left, directing you up the hill to the monastery.

New Skete Communities

Cambridge, NY

The term *skete,* originally the name of a remote settlement in the Egyptian desert, has come to mean a small, family-style monastic community with one spiritual father. New Skete belongs to the Orthodox Church in America led by His Beatitude, Theodosius, Archbishop of Washington and Metropolitan of All America and Canada.

In 1967, New Skete moved to 500 remote acres of steep, rocky land in northern New York State. The monks have built two beautifully crafted temples, both made of unfinished wood. The first, erected in 1970, is topped by gold cupolas or "onion" domes, giving the feeling of eastern Europe. The interior is adorned with Byzantine icons, many painted by the monks. This temple is always open to visitors. A few steps away is the second temple, dedicated in 1983 to Christ, the Wisdom of God. The floors are of Italian marble, and the furniture and altar screen are carved from ash, zebrawood, basswood, white oak, English brown oak—each piece a work of art. In the center of the altar stands the holy table of red oak, in which relics of martyrs are sealed as a reminder of the Church's baptism in blood. The high white walls give a sense of light-filled openness, and there are perfect acoustics. Given the rusticity of the outer structure and the remoteness of the location, this temple is like a jewel on a mountaintop.

New Skete is three separate communities governed by one spiritual leader. Each community has separate quarters and works to contribute its skills for the good of the whole. The monks have their living quarters next to the main temple. Nearby is a separate guest house with room for six. Visitors are expected to join the community for prayer and meals. They can help with grounds maintenance, office, and kennel work (see below), but this is not required. The nuns of New Skete have their own convent a few miles away, where they bake world-class cheesecake that is sold in their shop or by mail order. The Companions of New Skete, the third group, are married couples who live in Emmaus House, a separate residence on the property. They follow a religious rule, living and working in community, worshipping daily with the monks and nuns, and support themselves by sewing, weaving, and some outside jobs.

For years New Skete monks have bred, raised, and trained German shepherd dogs, for which they are known worldwide. Their definitive book, *How to Be Your Dog's Best Friend,* has sold thousands of copies. The monks also run a thriving mail-order business selling cured meats like ham, bacon, and sausage, plus cheeses and condiments.

The quality of their food products is reflected in their meals. Eating properly is as important at New Skete as praying and working well. The communities believe and practice that spirituality is a lived experience rather than a perceived one. As one monk said, "Having to care for other human beings roots you in spirituality."

New Skete Communities
P.O. Box *128*
Cambridge, NY *12816*
(518) 677-3928

Accommodations: *6 men, women, and children can be housed here, but only by reservation in advance with the guestmaster; delicious food; attendance at services and meals required; 500 acres; closed Mondays and for community retreats; $30 a night.*

Directions: *Cambridge is 1 hour northeast of Albany. From I-87 (Northway) take Exit 7 and drive east to Hoosic Falls, to Rte. 22 North to the town of Cambridge. Turn right at the only traffic light in town onto East Main St.; drive 3 miles east, and turn right onto Chestnut Hill Rd. Drive 1 mile and turn left onto New Skete Rd. Take this to the top of the mountain; the road ends at the monastery church and gift shop.*

Our Lady of the Resurrection Monastery

La Grangeville, NY

In a secluded area of Dutchess County, 22 acres of hilltop land are the site of a rambling wooden Benedictine monastery. It was founded by Brother Victor-Antoine d'Avila-Latourette, who had a vision of how a monk should live. The result is a beautiful and simple place that continually reminds one of man's connection to prayer, nature, art, and spirituality. A small flock of sheep keep the grass under control around the monastery and guesthouse; an herb and flower garden provides joy to the eye and zest to the cooking; the bedrooms are decorated with warm colors, and the living and dining rooms resemble a French country farmhouse. The chapel was constructed from stones found in the fields.

Brother Victor, who holds degrees in music, psychology, and education, was inspired by Father Peter Minard, a hermit and ascetic who seemed to him a living icon. Victor felt called to this simple way of life, following the duties and obligations of the Benedictine rules of hospitality, counsel, compassion, and concern for the environment.

The chapel has a European flavor, and the design and decorative touches are those of a master. Daily prayer services are held here, morning, noon, and evening. Both Gregorian chant and High

Church Slavonic are used in the services. Meals are taken in the refectory, whose windows and skylight look out to the trees and grounds. The food is delicious, and many of the recipes can be found in Brother Victor's popular cookbook, *From a Monastery Kitchen.* Guests can stay either in the monastery, where there are a few single rooms, or in the plain St. Scholastica Guest House, which has a separate kitchen for pick-up breakfast and snacks. Guesthouse visitors come to the monastery for lunch and supper. An excellent library is available. There is one hermitage set off in the woods for anyone wanting to be completely alone.

The monastery is devoted to contemplation and simplicity. Each person will approach this in a different way, but the monastery provides an opportunity for all to rest and withdraw for a while, to escape the noise and busy-ness of their lives.

Our Lady of the Resurrection Monastery
Barmore Rd.
La Grangeville, NY 12540

Accommodations: *For men and women, 6 beds in the guesthouse and 5–6 in the main house, plus a hermitage. Delicious meals prepared by the author of* From a Monastery Kitchen *cookbook; 4 cats, 2 dogs, 11 sheep; walks on rural roads; work possible on the farm or in the gardens; nice gift shop; usually closed January and February.*

Write to the guestmaster for reservations, price, and directions.

Our Lady's Guest and Retreat House Graymoor

Garrison, NY

The history of Graymoor goes back more than 100 years, to 1875, when the first building, St. John's Church, was erected on this steep hillside. In the early 1900s, Our Lady's Guest and Retreat House was built near the stuccoed church. It was used initially as a hospital and guesthouse, and then as a convent for the Franciscan Sisters of the Atonement. Retreats were first given here in 1920, and it continues today as a haven for those seeking a place for quiet reflection.

The retreat house has immense charm, with beautifully crafted dark woodwork from the original construction. The rooms have been carefully maintained and are comfortably furnished. There are sitting and meeting rooms on the main floor, and in the dining room the delicious food is prepared and served buffet-style by the resident sisters. The Sisters of the Atonement believe this is a special place of peace and comfort; it is here that their missionary nuns return for rest and renewal.

The second floor has small, comfortable single rooms for more than fifty guests, who share communal bathrooms. The rooms have single beds and a desk with chair. The chapel, St. John's Church, is a few steps away, and mass is said there daily; part of the original Graymoor complex, it has been added to, renovated, and refurbished.

Graymoor was founded in 1898 as an Anglican religious community for men and women. The founders took the name Society of the Atonement, dividing the word *atonement* into syllables—at-one-ment—which expressed the community's mission to promote Christian unity and to fulfill Jesus' prayer "that all may be one." In the spirit of unity, in 1909 the Society joined the Catholic Church. This was the first time since the days of the Reformation that an entire religious community became Catholic.

The retreat house makes the facilities available for diverse religious purposes and groups. The 1990 schedule lists weekend retreat meetings for Lutherans, Methodists, Charismatic Healing, and lay Franciscans. Private retreatants are welcome by arrangement, and spiritual counseling is available.

The work at Graymoor is far-reaching. Up the hill is a separate facility, St. Christopher's Inn, where alcoholics are housed and helped toward rehabilitation. Farther up the hill is St. Paul's Friary, a huge building, where priests and brothers of the Friars of Atonement live, do retreat work separately from the sisters, and occasionally welcome as overnight guests hikers on the Appalachian Trail, which runs just behind their building.

Our Lady's Guest and Retreat House
Graymoor
Rte. *9*
Garrison, NY *10524*
(914) 424-3300 ***(Our Lady)***
(914) 424-3671 ***(Friary)***

Accommodations: *Men and women are housed in 51 singles in the main house and in 2 smaller adjoining houses; 2 suites and rooms for 3 couples; delicious home-cooked, buffet-style meals; the Friary has beds for 40; a leg of the Appalachian Trail adjoins this extensive property; open year-round except Christmas and one week in summer; suggested donation: $30 a day, $75 a weekend.*

Directions: *Graymoor is located on Rte. 9 in Garrison, 4 miles north of Peekskill and 13 miles south of Fishkill. It is approximately 1 hour and 15 minutes from New York City, and the turnoff is on the right as you drive north. Our Lady's Guest House is the first building you come to (on the left) after you enter the drive.*

The Priory
Chestertown, NY

The Priory was built in the late 1970s on 100 hilltop acres as a Benedictine monastery, and is currently run by a small community of nuns who live here and offer the facilities to spiritually motivated groups.

Reminiscent of a ski chalet, the Priory has beds for guests in windowed sleeping nooks that look out on the Adirondack Mountains. There is a large chapel and a small meditation room, a spacious, efficient kitchen, and a large living room heated by a woodstove.

A committed group of laypeople nearby have taken responsibility for helping to manage the property to sustain this atmosphere of solitude and mountain quiet. The hilltop offers seclusion and tranquil views to the north and east.

There is a stable of program directors who give regular one-day and weekend retreats geared to helping individuals pause to reflect on spirituality and personal growth. These retreats are scheduled throughout the year and include a weekend in which visitors are invited to help spruce up the property: "Come to work, play, and pray."

The Priory
***P.O. Box** 336*
***Chestertown, NY** 12817*
(518) 494-3733

Accommodations: *For men, women, and children, 16 beds in singles and doubles; home-cooked communal meals; 100 acres for walking and cross-country skiing; Loon Lake nearby for swimming; open year-round; $25 a night.*

Directions: *From I-87 (Northway) take Exit 25, go 4.7 miles west to Charlie Fish Rd., and turn left on Priory Rd.*

St. Cuthbert's Retreat House

Brewster, NY

In 1959 a group of Episcopalian nuns of the Community of the Holy Spirit discovered this property on a quiet country road with dry-stone walls. The nuns had been searching for a country retreat house where they could find some respite from the strenuous life of teaching and administering their New York City school. The neighbors soon became used to seeing the nuns go back and forth in Beulah, their old Buick convertible with the gleaming chrome teeth. The car had a leaky top, so when it rained the nuns would open up their umbrellas inside the car to keep their habits dry.

On this 127 acres of woods and fields is the original farm—now called St. Cuthbert's—owned by the Sears family from 1810 to 1940. In the mid-1800s, after a trip to the West Indies, the senior Sears decided to build a veranda and a mansard roof, which meant adding a third story. The spacious and well-made house was ideal for the nuns, and it has been beautifully restored. The rooms still have 19th-century furnishings, and there are rumors of a friendly ghost who can be heard occasionally walking up the stairs during the day.

It seemed a natural step to open a day school here, as a means of supporting the country place, and to carry out the order's mission to educate. In the early 1960s the nuns founded Melrose, with a few grades of elementary school, and by 1970 they had to construct an entire building to accommodate the more than 100 students, from kindergarten to eighth grade. A convent wing was added to the new school building, and the nuns now live there.

Just across the road is the more modern St. Aidan's, which is used for smaller groups and private retreatants who want a few days in a beautiful country setting.

Morning and evening prayers are offered by the community in two chapels: one, used year-round, is in the school; the other, just behind St. Cuthbert's and used mainly in mild weather, is a charming wooden prayer house, like a giant gazebo.

The nuns who live and work here have managed to establish a successful educational program for the young while fulfilling their desire for a spiritual life. It is this place and time for meditation and prayer that they share with retreatants.

St. Cuthbert's Retreat House
Federal Hill Rd.
***Brewster, NY** 10509*
(914) 278-2610

Accommodations: *Singles and doubles for men and women, 17 beds at St. Cuthbert's and 8 at St. Aidan's; meals prepared at St. Cuthbert's; community prayer; 127 acres; can arrange work on property; open year-round; suggested donation: $50 a night.*

Directions: *From New York City, take the Saw Mill Pkwy. to where it merges with I-684 North. Follow I-684 to Rte. 22 (as if to Pawling,* not *the first Brewster exit). After passing Heidi's Motel and a temple, at the traffic light turn right onto Milltown Rd. Pass a cemetery and a small bridge, then turn right immediately onto Federal Hill Rd. (watch for* MELROSE SCHOOL *sign). The retreat house is on the right.*

St. Francis Center

Oyster Bay, NY

Located on the Gold Coast of Long Island, that stretch of the northern shore where there is one magnificent estate after another, St. Francis Center is one of those posh paradises with which affluent people displayed their wealth in the early 1900s. In erecting this Italianate villa, the Sanderson family spared no expense. In 1915 they hired the architect who designed the Vanderbilt mansion on Fifth Avenue in New York City and the landscapers of New York's Central Park. They brought in Italian stone artists and German artisans to make the inside like a European palace. The main rooms retain that singular workmanship, and the entire building, despite the large number of rooms, has a sense of grand intimacy.

The property was eventually willed to the Glen Cove Community Hospital and bought from them in 1960 by the Franciscan Brothers of Brooklyn, who came to the United States from Ireland in 1854. The brothers teach primarily at St. Francis College and a few Long  Island high schools. They also do social work and prison ministry, and have used the center for their own retreats. Although they do not organize retreats, they have expanded the use of the facility for groups of up to 50, and provide meals and general maintenance. The center has been used by such organizations as Amnesty International and Transcendental Meditation, as well as for yoga, marriage encounters, and youth and college prayer groups.

There is a large, comfortable chapel—the former living room—as well as a dining room with huge fireplaces, cast-bronze doors, and ornamented walls and ceilings. There are several large rooms for meetings as well as a library and sitting rooms.

The 25 surrounding acres ensure privacy. Around the mansion are terraces, fountains, statues, and a grotto, all kept in remarkable condition considering the size of the work force, namely one Franciscan brother with part-time help.

This is an imposing and beautiful place for a group to gather in seclusion.

St. Francis Center
Planting Field Rd.
Oyster Bay, NY *11771*
(516) 922-3708

Accommodations: *For men and women, 50 beds in 21 singles, doubles, and triples; open only on weekends to groups of 30–50; family-style meals; 25 acres of gardens and lawns, with a 415-acre state arboretum across the road; open year-round; $100 a weekend.*

Directions: *From the Long Island Expressway, take Exit 41N. Drive north on Rte. 106 for 3 miles and turn left on Rte. 25A (Northern Blvd.). At the first traffic light (3/10 mile), turn right onto Mill River Rd. Proceed 2 miles to Glen Cove–Oyster Bay Rd. and turn left. After 1/2 mile, turn left again onto Planting Field Rd. The center is 1/2 mile along, on the right. Drive to the main building. (Watch for the green-and-white Arboretum signs; St. Francis is on the right, 1/4 mile past the Arboretum, which is on the left.)*

St. Gabriel's Retreat House

Shelter Island, NY

Since the early 1960s, the Catholic Passionist priests and brothers have held retreats for young people at their 35-acre waterfront Shelter Island property. About 2,500 teenagers come each year for long weekends and the chance to step back a little and examine their relationships with God and with other people. One man who works here and at Covenant House, a youth crisis center in New York City, said, "We want kids here so we don't get them at Covenant House."

The property looks out over Coecles Harbor, and features a large outdoor swimming pool as well as ocean bathing, fields for baseball and soccer, and plenty of room to roam. The retreatants have single rooms with sinks and community washrooms. Meals are cafeteria-style, taken in a large dining room. The chapel shown above is where prayer services are held.

The average size of the groups is 42, and the age range is 14 to 18. The schedule is organized around talks dealing with knowing oneself, God and prayer, guided meditation, sexuality, family, and reconciliation. After each talk there are small group meetings to examine the topics further.

This is a great place for city kids to get a chance to see another perspective, to experience a spiritual awakening, and to learn from committed people the importance of cooperation in dealing with others. There are separate accommodations for up to ten adults.

St. Gabriel's Retreat House
64 ***Burns Rd., P.O. Box P***
Shelter Island, NY *11965*
(516) 749-0850

Accommodations: *For youths, 55 singles; rooms for 5–6 adults in the House of Prayer (a 185-year-old farmhouse) and 3–4 in the bungalow; cafeteria dining; kitchen in the House of Prayer; open year-round (August for Passionists); $75–$100 a weekend.*

Directions: *Take the Shelter Island Ferry from either North Haven or Greenport to Rte. 114 (Cartwright Rd.) to Burns Rd. Turn right on Burns Rd. to St. Gabriel's. (If coming from Greenport, turn left on Burns Rd.)*

St. Joseph Spiritual Life Center

Valatie, NY

The Catholic Brothers of the Holy Cross have been here in the Hudson River valley since 1935, when the Farrell family bequeathed their manor house and 190 acres to the order. Over the years, to protect their solitude, the brothers have acquired another 200 acres and now own over 400 acres of surrounding woodlands, farmlands, meadows, and orchards.

Their spacious building, formerly used to house and educate novices, has rooms for 50 retreatants, mostly twin beds in clean, spare rooms with sinks and community bathrooms. There is a conference room and a lounge as well as small parlors and meeting rooms. A large and beautiful chapel at one end of the house is elegantly decorated. The muted light filtering through its narrow stained-glass windows throws a patina of rainbow colors on the high white walls.

The mission of the center is to provide programs for both adults and youths in search of spiritual growth. The brothers have a series of directed retreats, many around the church calendar of Advent, Lent, and Holy Week. The center also makes the facility available to outside groups.

The Brothers of the Holy Cross were founded in Montreal in the 19th century by Basil Moreau, the spiritual director of Brother André, who was beatified by Pope John Paul II in May 1982. Brother

André, despite fragile health, lived to be 92. Because he experienced so much illness in his own life, André had great compassion for other sufferers. He often anointed the sick with oil from the vigil light that burned before the altar of St. Joseph. Many cures were attributed to this ritual and André's prayers, and he became known as "the miracle man of Montreal." When people claimed he had cured them, André would always insist, "I do not cure. St. Joseph cures."

The brothers here feel an affinity with their founder and with Brother André. In all their work the brothers emphasize the fundamental purpose of religious life, which is the union of the individual soul with God.

St. Joseph Spiritual Life Center
RD 5, Box 113
Valatie, NY 12184
(518) 784-9481

Accommodations: *Single and double rooms for 85 men and women; cafeteria meals; 400 acres for hiking or cross-country skiing; tennis courts and pond; closed 2 weeks in August; $35 a night.*

Directions: *From the east on I-90, take Exit B1; from the west on I-90, take Exit 12. Drive south on U.S. 9 for 3 miles, and turn right at Maple Lane. The Center is on the right.*

From the south, take I-87 (New York State Thruway) to Exit 21A (Berkshire Spur). Follow this to Exit B1. From there, take U.S. 9 as above.

From New York City and Connecticut, take the Taconic Pkwy. to Rte. 203 (Chatham). Follow Rte. 203 West to U.S. 9, and drive north on U.S. 9 about 4 miles. Turn left at Maple Lane. The Center is on the right.

St. Mary's Villa
Sloatsburg, NY

In the early 20th century, Italian masons used stone found on this property to build a magnificent English Gothic mansion for the descendants of Alexander Hamilton. Located at Table Rock in the foothills of the Ramapo Mountains, on 200 acres of cleared fields and woods, it is now a spiritual and educational center for the Congregation of the Sisters Servants of Mary Immaculate of the Eastern Catholic Rite. The main house, all 52 rooms and 4 stories of it, is still in remarkably good condition. There are fireplaces in every main room, including most bathrooms; there were originally wine and coal cellars, offices for the family, and rooms on the fourth floor for staff. The nuns who live here and maintain this grand place acquired the property in 1942, used it as a girls' school for many years, and then turned it into a retreat center.

These Ukrainian Catholic nuns, known for their hospitality and fine cooking, make their facilities available for youth and adult retreats, and corporate meetings or seminars. They also welcome individuals for private retreats for a quiet day of reflection, a weekend, or a longer stay.

The indoor chapel is the former main dining room, a beautifully wood-paneled room decorated with icons. An outstanding painting behind the altar shows the Dormition of the Mother of God. The community meets here four times a day to sing the liturgy, and retreatants are always welcome.

The house has walls and floors of oak, and the ceilings are elaborately sculptured plaster. At the end of one of the main rooms is a large Norman-style fireplace that dominates the entire wall. Along the south side is an enclosed porch with leaded-glass windows and redwood trim. This offers a fine view of Sheppard Pond down the hill. The bedrooms are comfortable and clean, most with shared bath. The corridors in one sleeping wing were finished with hand-painted wallpaper that is still in good condition, though it is over 80 years old.

There is an annual pilgrimage of almost 6,000 people to St. Mary's, the Sunday on or before August 15, the Feast of the Assumption. By midmorning 60 to 70 priests are hearing the confessions of those already assembled on the grounds. This feast is an important one for the Ukrainian Church, and St. Mary's has become a special place for the community to gather.

St. Mary's Villa
Table Rock
Sloatsburg, NY *10974*
(914) 753-5100

Accommodations: *Singles and doubles for 65 men and women; American and Ukrainian cusine; 200 acres of natural trails; swimming pool; tennis court; daily mass; open year-round, though July and August are reserved mainly for the use of the nuns; $25 a night.*

Directions: *Located 1 hour from New York City. Take Rte. 17 North to the Ringwood exit (Sterling Mine Rd.). Continue approximately 2 miles and turn left to St. Mary's Villa at the* ST. JOSEPH'S HOME *sign. Proceed 7/10 mile to main building.*

Springwater Center

Springwater, NY

The Springwater Center began in 1982, when Toni Packer, then abbot of the Rochester Zen Center, left with a group of students to form the Genesee Valley Zen Center. Subsequently, the name was changed to Springwater Center for Meditative Inquiry and Retreats. The new center, as Toni Packer explains, was born out of the need to question the forms of inherited Zen practice and the authority vested in religious teachers and traditions. This process of inquiry has continued to shape the activity of the center, responding to the needs of people working together, both in and out of retreats. Here an attempt is being made to adapt the practice of Zen to Western society. Most of the traditional forms have been dropped. For example, *dokusan,* the formal interview between teacher and student, is now simply a "meeting." Some people work with koans, others do not; some work on the breath, others come up with a question that moves them. The *keisaku* (the stick administered during zazen to awaken drowsy students) is not used.

There is a spacious meditation room with tall windows that bathe the wood floors and walls in generous light. Other large rooms are used for exercise. There is a solarium and a large kitchen to accommodate many helpers. There are sleeping quarters for up to 50 people, many in dormitory style, and guests bring their own linens or a sleeping bag.

Retreats are scheduled regularly. Silence is observed throughout to provide the opportunity for introspection that is so difficult in an active, busy life. There are sitting periods, a daily talk, and individual meetings with the retreat directors, as well as communal work (meal preparation, house cleaning, and grounds maintenance). Except for the work periods, all activities are optional. Time is set aside for exercise and rest.

The property has ample space for walking, hiking, or cross-country skiing. One can explore the old farm ponds and buildings, or just find a quiet place beneath a tree. The center is on 200 acres in a beautifully remote section of western New York, yet within an hour's drive of Rochester. It has superb views of the surrounding hills and valley.

Springwater Center
7179 ***Mill St.***
Springwater, NY *14560*
(716) 669-2141

Accommodations: *Singles, doubles, or triples for 45 men and women; vegetarian meals; hot tub; exercise room; tape library; cross-country skiing; bird watching; open year round; $35 a night.*

Directions: *The Springwater Center is located about 40 miles south of Rochester. From I-90, take I-390 South. At Exit 9 (Lakeville/Conesus), drive south on Rte. 15 for about 18 miles; at this point there is a sign with flashing yellow lights at the side of the road. Take the next left off Rte. 15, which is Mill St. The Center is the third driveway on your left.*

Still Point House of Prayer

Stillwater, NY

Taking the name "Still Point" from T. S. Eliot's *Four Quartets,* in 1972 Dominican sister Sylvia Rosell wrote a proposal to her order for a house of prayer, seeking support for one year. After only six months, the venture became self-sufficient and her ministry of bringing life and prayer closer together continues to grow. Her directed and guided retreats are combined with holistic health programs, yoga, meditation (the Jesus prayer), and zazen, with some time for winter and summer sports.

Still Point is one of the quietest places imaginable. The 30-acre property appears neighborless, a spot completely overlooked by the rest of the world. The main building, Hospitality House—a reconditioned farmhouse—has space for seven to sleep in small, comfortable rooms. There is a chapel with a circular window behind the altar that looks out on the woods. Morning and evening prayer sessions include Matins at 7:30 A.M., and Vespers and meditation in the late afternoon, just before supper. A priest comes to say mass three times a week. Down the hall from the chapel is the dining-living room where guests meet to share an evening vegetarian meal. Breakfast and lunch are pick-up style in the kitchen.

There are five small hermitages off in the woods, a short walk from the main house. Those on hermitage retreat can take food back or join the other guests at the evening meal.

Just below the main house is a tranquil pond next to Meditation Park, a landscaped area with benches for quiet contemplation. Beyond the park, on a little hill, are outdoor Stations of the Cross and a Native American Medicine Wheel.

Still Point's focus is spiritual growth through the healing process of meditation, prayer, solitude, and quiet. The name of the community truly reflects its purpose. As Sister Sylvia says, "As soon as you stop the train, you can see what cargo you're carrying."

Still Point House of Prayer
***RD** 1*
***Stillwater, NY** 12170*
(518) 587-4967

Accommodations: *Open to men, women, and children as extended family; 7 in the main house, 5 hermits in 4 hermitages; pick-up breakfast and lunch and vegetarian dinner with the community; prayer, meditation, yoga; 30 acres with meditation park and Native American Medicine Wheel, pond; open year-round; suggested donation: $20 a night.*

Directions: *Still Point is 2.2 miles south of Saratoga Lake. From I-87 (Northway), take Exit 12 to U.S. 9 North, then take Rte. 9P East to Rte. 423, right on Rte. 423 for about 2.2 miles, then right on Land Fill Rd. to the end. Turn right up the drive.*

Transfiguration Monastery
Windsor, NY

In 1979 three Benedictine nuns joined together to live a simple monastic life on 100 acres of fields and woodland in the Susquehanna Valley, near Binghamton. One of these three, Sister Mary Placid, remembers back in 1930 meeting two young American boys who were taking apples from her backyard in her native France. The boys subsequently became her friends, and after she entered the convent she continued to pray for them. Years later, when she read *The Seven Storey Mountain,* she discovered that her childhood friends were Thomas Merton and his brother John Paul.

Both the monastery and the cozy guesthouse are built of logs and heated by woodstoves. The guesthouse has a kitchen where visitors may prepare their own breakfast with the basics provided. After noon prayer, there is a main meal in the monastery dining room with the community. This meal is taken in silence or accompanied by sacred music, but over dessert there is an opportunity for conversation with the gracious nuns. In the evening, prepared food is brought to the guest house kitchen in a picnic basket.

The community meets four times a day to sing the liturgy in the chapel, which is decorated with extraordinary icons. Guests are welcome at all services.

There is a golf course adjacent to the property, where one of the nuns regularly strolls the border, a good place to pray. If she finds a golf ball, she brings it back and adds it to the monastery's collection. These balls are cleaned, put into egg cartons, and sold back to the world, labeled "Holy in One." The sisters also make wine from their own grapes, which is bottled under the St. Benedict Winery label. One sister does superb icon painting, and periodically the monastery sponsors retreats and conferences. For a while the nuns operated a catering business, but this took them away from home too much. However, they still provide delicious food—French country-style—and it's worth a visit just for that. But there's more here. As one nun said, "A monastery is a sacred space for sacred time. People are attracted for that reason."

Transfiguration Monastery
***RD** 2, **Box** 2612*
***Windsor, NY** 13865*
(607) 655-2366

Accommodations: *For men, women, and children, singles and doubles for 10–11 in 2 guesthouses and a hermitage on 100 acres in the Susquehanna Valley; delicious French country cooking at the guesthouse in the evening and with the community in silence at noon; prayer four times daily; homemade wines and jellies; open year-round; $35 a night, or free-will donation.* 

Directions: *Located near Binghamton. From Rte. 17 take Exit 79 onto Rte. 79 South for 3 miles. The driveway for the monastery is just past the golf course sign on the right before you reach the course itself.*

Wellsprings

Glens Falls, NY

Founded in the mid 1980s in a former convent located in a quiet neighborhood, Wellsprings identifies itself as a Christian renewal center, and is run by the Catholic Sisters of St. Joseph of Carondelet. The only program offered is 4 months long, costs $4,000, and is for Christian ministers who want to revitalize their calling.

The format helps individuals assess their life and talents, examine their spiritual ministry, and then plan for the future. The length of the course provides the time, the atmosphere, and the encouragement to make all this possible.

There is a balanced series of presentations given by experts in the fields of theology, scripture, psychology, social justice, and effective living. Work is done in small groups, and adequate time is allowed for discussion, reflection, and integration of these ideas.

This is an advanced school of personal reflection in a supportive atmosphere, giving individuals the time and guidance to understand where they are and reflect on how to proceed. One participant saw it as "a balance between professional update and personal freedom for growth." Another described it as a "time to remember *me;* a chance to come home."

Wellsprings
93 Maple St.
***Glens Falls, NY** 12801*
(518) 792-3183

Accommodations: *Singles for 30 men and women who gather for a 4-month renewal program of communal living; walking, biking, skiing, and hiking are easily accessible; 2 sessions yearly; $4,000.*

Directions: *Glens Falls is about 40 miles north of Albany on I-87 (Northway). Wellsprings is located downtown in this small town.*

Zen Mountain Monastery

Mount Tremper, NY

Located deep in the Catskill Mountains, the 200 acres of nature sanctuary that make up the monastery grounds are bordered by the Beaverkill and Esopus rivers. The property is surrounded by thousands of acres of New York State Forest preserve and has miles of hiking trails. The main building, a well-crafted four-story stone structure built in the early 20th century, contains a large meditation hall, classrooms, a dining room, and a library. Here too are the sleeping quarters for guests and retreatants, in dormitories with communal bathrooms. Visitors should bring a sleeping bag or blanket, a towel, and loose, comfortable clothing for sitting and outside work.

Since the monastery opened ten years ago, it has become known for one of the most rigorous and authentic Zen training programs in the United States. Retreatants for weekend or week-long programs enter the routine of the monastery itself. The emphasis here is on practice rather than on formal teaching. Each activity provides a mirror to study the self, from the moment the wake-up bell sounds for early-morning zazen, followed by chanting and a ceremonial breakfast that provides an opportunity to observe the effect of the foods on the body, and so on throughout the day. Staff and guests work silently together doing caretaking, a practice of giving back to the buildings and grounds some of the benefits received from them.

All meals are taken buffet-style in the dining hall, and each person helps to clean up afterward. The afternoons are spent according to the retreat schedule, either with continuing work practice, classical Zen art and contemporary art, martial arts, or reading. The focus of each and every moment is the "still point" of Zen: the ultimate aim to make of one's life an expression of one's practice.

The concentrated simplicity of Zen is more than a philosophy; it is a way of life tracing back to the Buddha himself. The path of concentration development, through sitting zazen, helps bring body, breathing, and mind into harmony so that we may realize that we are not separate from other people. Neither are we limited to any one religion or cultural tradition. From this understanding, compassion and empathy for all human beings arises naturally.

Zen Mountain Monastery
Box 197 RB, South Plank Rd.
Mt. Tremper, NY 12457
(914) 688-2228

Accommodations: *For 45 men and women. Guests stay in dormitories in the monastery. Private rooms and cabins are for monks, staff, and long-term program attendees. Vegetarian meals; work required of all guests; open year-round; $35 a night.*

Directions: *Located 120 miles north of New York City and 80 miles south of Albany. From I-87 (New York State Thruway) take Exit 19 (Kingston). At the traffic circle, take Rte. 28 West (Pine Hill) for 20 miles to the junction of Rte. 212 on the right. Take Rte. 212 to the first 4-way intersection; turn left. The monastery gate is on the right, a block after the turn.*

New York: Other Places

Camp Pioneer (Lutheran), 9324 Lakeshore Rd., **Angola,** NY 14006. (716) 549-1420

Camp Ma-He-Tu, **Bear Mountain,** NY 10911 (914) 351-4508. Mailing address: 231 Madison Ave., **New York,** NY 10016. (212) 696-6771

St. Ursula Center, Middle Rd., **Blue Point,** NY 11715. (516) 363-2422

Barry House, Rte. 8, **Brant Lake,** NY 12815. (518) 494-3314

Cursillos Center, 118 Congress St., **Brooklyn,** NY 11201. (718) 624-5670

St. Paul's Center, 484 Humboldt St., **Brooklyn,** NY 11211. (718) 389-0155

Community of the Way of the Cross Retreat Center, 4588 S. Park Ave., **Buffalo,** NY 14219. (716) 823-8877

Notre Dame Retreat House, P.O. Box 342, Foster Rd., **Canandaigua,** NY 14424. (716) 394-5700

Lily Dale Metaphysical Assembly, 5 Melrose Park, **Cassadaga,** NY 14752. (716) 595-8721

Thornfield Conference Center, West Lake Rd., Box 38, **Cazenovia,** NY 13035. (315) 655-3123

St. Mary's Mission Center, 28 Oak St., **Champlain,** NY 12919. (518) 298-3503

Bellinger Hall, Chautauqua Institution, **Chautauqua,** NY 14722. (716) 357-6213

Center for Christian Living, 10324 Main St., **Clarence,** NY 14031. (716) 759-6454

St. Ignatius Renewal Center, 6969 Strickler Rd., **Clarence Center,** NY 14032. (716) 741-3811

Vanderkamp, Martin Road, **Cleveland,** NY 13042. (315) 675-3651

Grail Conference Center, 119 Duncan Ave., P.O. Box 475, **Cornwall-on-Hudson,** NY 12520. (914) 534-8495

Pumpkin Hollow Farm, RR 1, P.O. Box 135, **Craryville,** NY 12521. (518) 325-3583

St. Columban Center, 6892 Lake Shore Rd., P.O. Box 816, **Derby,** NY 14047. (716) 947-4708

New York City Mission Society, **Dover Plains,** NY 12522. (914) 832-6151

Monastery of Mary the Queen, 1310 W. Church St., **Elmira,** NY 14905.

Marist Brothers Retreat House, P.O. Box 186, **Esopus,** NY 12429. (914) 384-6620

St. Francis Retreat House, Fonda Kateri Shrine, P.O. Box 627, **Fonda,** NY 12068. (518) 853-3646

Emmanuel Christian Church Retreat House, Retreat House Rd., **Glenmont,** NY 12077. (518) 463-1296

Salesian Center for Youth Ministry, 334 Main St., **Goshen,** NY 10924. (914) 294-5138

Camp Epworth, **High Falls,** NY 12440. (914) 687-0215. Mailing address: 252 Bryant Ave., White Plains, NY 10605. (914) 997-1570

Bethany Retreat House, County Road 105, **Highland Mills,** NY 10930. (914) 928-2213

Presbyterian Center at Holmes, 183 Denton Lake Road, **Holmes,** NY 12531. (914) 878-6383

Wilbur Herrlich Retreat Center, P.O. Box 59, RFD, **Holmes,** NY 12531. (914) 878-6662. Mailing address: 585 Townline Road, Hauppauge, NY 11787. (516) 265-1183

Bishop Molloy Passionist Retreat House, 86-45 178th St., **Jamaica Estates,** NY 11432. (718) 739-1229

Holy Trinity Monastery, **Jordanville,** NY 13361. (315) 858-0940

Trinity Retreat, 1 Pryer Manor Rd., **Larchmont,** NY 10538. (914) 235-6839

Cenacle Retreat House, Center for Spiritual Renewal, 310 Cenacle Rd., **Lake Ronkonkoma,** NY 11779. (516) 588-8366

Monastery of Bethlehem, **Livingston Manor,** NY 12758. (914) 439-4300

Beaver Camp, Number 4 Rd., **Lowville,** NY 13367. (315) 376-2640

Unirondack, Inc., Star Rte. 4, **Lowville,** NY 13367. (315) 376-6888. Mailing address: 220 South Winton Rd., Rochester, NY 14610. (716) 473-3301

St. Ignatius Retreat House, Searington Rd., **Manhasset,** NY 11030. (516) 621-8300

Maryknoll Mission Institute, P.O. Box 529, **Maryknoll,** NY 10545. (914) 941-7575

Ananda Ashram, RD 3, P.O. Box 141, **Monroe,** NY 10950. (914) 782-5575

House of Holy Innocents, 772 Mt. Sinai Corem Rd., **Mount Sinai,** NY 11766. (516) 331-1745

Little Portion Friary, P.O. Box 399, **Mount Sinai,** NY 11766-0399. (516) 473-0553

Matagiri, **Mount Tremper,** NY 12457. (914) 679-8322

Our Lady of Hope Center, 434 River Rd., **Newburgh,** NY 12550. (914) 561-0685

St. Margaret's House, Jordan Rd., **New Hartford,** NY 13413. (315) 724-2324

Discovery Jewish Heritage Seminars, 1220 Broadway, No. 610, **New York,** NY 10019. (212) 643-8800 (for retreats in New York and other states)

Hadassah "Kallahs," Jewish Education Dept., 50 West 58th St. **New York,** NY 10019. (for retreats in New York and other states)

St. Joseph's Cursillo Center, 523 West 142 St., **New York,** NY 10031. (212) 926-7433

Powell House, RD 1, P.O. Box 160, **Old Chatham,** NY 12136. (518) 294-8811

Mariandale Dominican Sisters, Dominican Reflection Center, P.O. Box 231, Rte. 9, **Ossining,** NY 10562 (914) 941-4455

Watson Homestead Conference and Retreat Center, P.O. Box 168, Dry Run Road, **Painted Post,** NY 14870. (607) 962-0541

Sisters of the Good Shepherd Spiritual Center, Mount Florence, Maple Ave., **Peekskill,** NY 10566. (914) 339-4488

St. Mary's Convent and Retreat House, John St., **Peekskill,** NY 10566. (914) 739-5387

Pathwork Center, P.O. Box 66, **Phoenicia,** NY 12464. (914) 688-2211

Regina Maria Retreat House, 77 Brinkerhoff St., **Plattsburgh,** NY 12901. (518) 561-3421

Metropolitan Baptist Camp, RFD 1, **Poughquag,** NY 12570. (914) 724-5295. Mailing address: c/o American Baptist Camps, 225 Park Ave. South, New York, NY 10003. (212) 254-0880

Cardinal Spellman Retreat House, 5801 Palisade Ave., **Riverdale,** NY 10471. (212) 549-6500

Cenacle Center for Spiritual Renewal, 693 East Ave., **Rochester,** NY 14607. (716) 271-8755 or (716) 271-8791

Holy Family House of Prayer, 980 North Village Ave., **Rockville Centre,** NY 11570. (516) 766-2044

Wainwright House, 260 Stuyvesant Ave., **Rye,** NY 10580. (914) 967-6080

Arrowood, Anderson Hill Rd., **Rye Brook,** NY 10573. (914) 939-5500

Maycroft, **Sag Harbor,** NY 11963. (516) 725-1181

Resurrection House, 20 River St., **Saranac Lake,** NY 12983. (518) 891-1182

Dominican Retreat House, 1945 Union St., **Schenectady,** NY 12309. (518) 393-4169

Stella Maris Retreat Center, 130 East Genesee St., **Skaneateles,** NY 13152. (315) 685-6836

SYDA Foundation, P.O. Box 600, **South Fallsburg,** NY 12779. (914) 434-2000

Rune Hill, RD 2, **Spencer,** NY 14883. (607) 589-6392

Beaver Cross Camp, P.O. Box 218, **Springfield Center,** NY 13468. (607) 547-9489

Mount Manresa, 239 Fingerboard Rd., **Staten Island,** NY 10305. (718) 727-3844

Center of Renewal, 4421 Lower River Rd., **Stella Niagara,** NY 14144. (716) 754-4314

Stony Point Center, Crickettown Rd., **Stony Point,** NY 10980. (914) 786-3734

Bethany House, 806 Court St., **Syracuse,** NY 13208. (315) 472-4638

Christ the King Retreat House, 500 Brookford Rd., **Syracuse,** NY 13224. (315) 446-2680

Island Retreat, Bluff Island, **Tupper Lake,** NY 12986. (518) 359-7473, or (606) 586-7242 (Sept.–May)

Convent of St. Helena, P.O. Box 426, **Vails Gate,** NY 12584. (914) 562-0592

Camp De Wolfe, Northside Rd., **Wading River,** NY 11792. (516) 929-4325. Mailing address: 36 Cathedral Ave., Garden City, NY 11530

St. Andrew's House, 89A St. Andrew's Rd., **Walden,** NY 12586. (914) 778-3707

Deer Hill Conference and Retreat Center, Wheeler Hill Rd., RD 1, **Wappingers Falls,** NY 12590. (914) 297-2323

Mount Alvernia Retreat House, P.O. Box 858, **Wappingers Falls,** NY 12590. (914) 297-5707

Skye Farm Camps, Schroon River Rd., **Warrensburg,** NY 12885. (518) 494-2137

Mount Alverno Center, 20 Grand St., **Warwick,** NY 10990. (914) 986-2267

Warwick Conference Center, Inc., P.O. Box 349, **Warwick,** NY 10990. (914) 986-1164

Cabrini-on-the-Hudson, Rte. 9W, **West Park,** NY 12493. (914) 384-6720

Wise Woman Center, P.O. Box 64, **Woodstock,** NY 12498. (914) 246-8081

Beaver Conference Farm, Underhill Ave., RD 3, **Yorktown Heights,** NY 10598. (914) 962-6033

Inn of the Spirit, Washington Lake Rd., **Yulan,** NY 12792. (914) 557-8145

The greatest people in the world have passed away unknown. The Buddhas and the Christs that we know are but second-rate heros in comparison with the greatest of whom the world knows nothing. Hundreds of these unknown heros have lived in every country working silently. Silently they live and silently they pass away, and in time their thoughts find expression in Buddhas or Christs; and it is these latter that become known to us. The highest people do not seek to get any name or fame from their knowledge. They leave their ideas to the world; they put forth no claims for themselves and establish no schools or systems in their name. Their whole nature shrinks from such a thing . . . the highest are calm, silent and unknown. They really know the power of thought; they are sure that even if they go into a cave and close the door and simply think five true thoughts and then pass away, these five thoughts of theirs will live throughout eternity. Indeed, such thoughts of theirs will penetrate through the mountains, cross the oceans and travel through the world. They will enter deep into human hearts and brains and raise up men and women who will give them practical expression in the workings of human life. . . .

SWAMI VIVEKANANDA

Pennsylvania

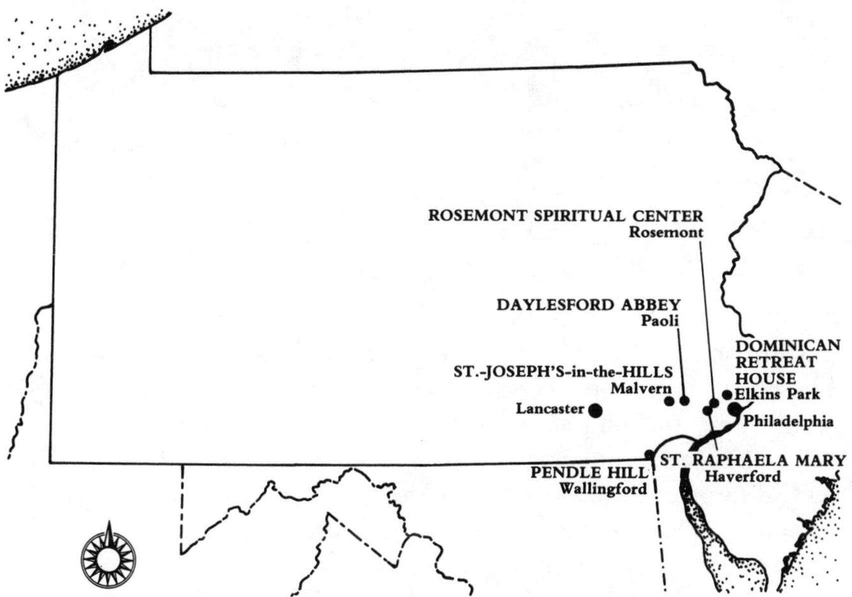

Daylesford Abbey
Paoli, PA

At the center of 120 acres of beautiful lawns and fields is a large, modern abbey church where well-attended Sunday services are held. There is a small chapel beside the main church where the Norbertine monks pray morning and evening and guests are welcome. Behind the church and connected to it is a three-story building that has several large meeting rooms on the first floor, a seminary on the second, and rooms for 35 retreatants on the third.

There is a small house called Emmaus for private retreats or small groups, set away from the main complex. It has two small chapels, a kitchen-dining area stocked with basics, and five bedrooms with two baths. Nearby, through the trees and across a meadow, is a lovely hermitage, and behind that a pond with an exquisite stone chapel for prayer and meditation.

The abbey serves the community by administering and teaching in local schools, providing parish priests, and supporting facilities in Philadelphia for homeless men and women. It also sends chaplains to local hospitals and conducts retreats and programs dedicated to religious and cultural renewal.

While making their facilities available for private retreats and outside groups, the Norbertines themselves offer a series of retreat evenings and weekends ranging from programs of investigative reading on works of Christian mystics to workshops on the Enneagram, exploring the motivation of thought and action.

The Order of Premontre, founded by Saint Norbert in 12th-century France, established its first successful American community in Wisconsin, working with immigrants from Holland, Belgium, and France. The Norbertines founded parishes and schools and soon attracted young Americans into their communities. From these new monks a group moved to Delaware in 1932, and two years later, at the request of the diocese, the Norbertines came to Philadelphia as teachers. In 1954 a group came to Paoli and founded Daylesford Abbey. These Catholic priests and brothers are sworn to seek Christ through community living, poverty, obedience, celibacy, and a dedication to the ministry. The underlying belief is that an active religious life needs an ascetic and contemplative haven, and this is what the abbey offers, not only to its residents but to visitors as well.

Daylesford Abbey
220 ***S. Valley Rd.***
Paoli, PA *19301*
(215) 647-2530

Accommodations: *Singles and doubles in the abbey for 50–55 men and women; 5-bedroom guesthouse; hermitage; well-stocked kitchens in the guesthouse and hermitage; dining with the community in the abbey; morning prayer, mass, Vespers daily; 130 beautifully landscaped acres; closed mid-August for cleaning and renovation; suggested donation: $35 a night.*

Directions: *From Washington, D.C., take I-95 to 320 North near Wilmington to 252 North; turn left through Media to Newtown Square to Rte. 30; pass St. Norbert Parish, left on U.S. 30, 2 lights and left onto Valley Rd.; drive 1 mile; abbey sign is on the right. From Philadelphia, take I-76 West to Rte. 202 South. Take this to exit for Paoli. This is 252 South. Continue until intersection with Rte. 30 (Lancaster Pike). Turn right onto Rte. 30 and left onto Valley Rd. at second traffic light. The Abbey is 1 mile farther on the right.*

Dominican Retreat House

Elkins Park, PA

The first glimpse of the main house is imposing: The 45-room structure resembles a European chateau. It was built in 1903 by William Elkins, a wealthy Philadelphian who commissioned Horace Trumbauer, the architect of the Widener Library at Harvard and the Philadelphia Free Library. Trumbauer created a masterpiece in granite and Indiana limestone in the style of the Italian Renaissance.

The main entry, through giant bronze doors, leads into a room of marble floors and pillars. Massive chandeliers hang down from 20-foot-high ceilings that are painted with murals so that every corner has some elegant decoration. There is a comfortable, wood-paneled library and a music room decorated in gold leaf and painted in pastel colors that reflect the light.

The central staircase leads to the former art gallery, now the retreatants' chapel, a cozy room with a frosted skylight and marble columns. The Stations of the Cross in this chapel and another are hand-carved wooden figures. Other spacious rooms on the main floor, formerly a breakfast room and dining room, are now used for discussions and lectures.

A wing of 84 rooms, where retreatants stay, was added in 1960. The rooms are comfortable, each with a single bed, a desk, a reading lamp, a small closet, and a window that looks out on the beautiful grounds. The complex has acres of well-kept lawns, gardens, shrubs, and trees. From the main house the road and pathways lead to St. Dominic's and Gregory Hall, two other buildings that add to the sense of grandeur. There are lakes to visit, outdoor Stations of the Cross, a Fatima shrine, and a Lourdes grotto. Near the front gate is a shrine to Saint Joseph. There is even a greenhouse where flowers and plants are cultivated throughout the year.

The property was acquired from the Elkins family by Dominican nuns in 1932. The sisters have restored a private showplace and made it accessible to thousands who enjoy the grand setting while attending the popular weekend retreats. Retreats deal with topics of alcohol and drugs, separation or divorce, and midlife direction. Or one can simply spend a weekend of silent contemplation in a lovely, restful setting.

Dominican Retreat House
750 ***Ashbourne Rd.***
Elkins Park, PA *19117*
(215) 782-8520; 224-0945

Accommodations: *For men and women, 84 modern singles in new wing and 22 bedrooms in main house; cottages on property; simple buffet-style meals; daily mass; 42 acres of lush, spacious grounds, gardens, ponds; library; open year-round except Christmas and Easter; $35 a night.*

Directions: *From I-276 (Pennsylvania Turnpike), take the Willow Grove exit and follow Rte. 611 South through Willow Grove, Abington, and Jenkintown to Elkins Park. Ashbourne Rd. (picket fence at corner) is located at the fourth traffic light after Church Rd. Turn right on Ashbourne Rd.; the Retreat House is at the first intersection on the left.*

Or *(also from I-276) take the Fort Washington exit and follow Rte.* 309 *South* 5 1/2 *miles. Turn left at the end of the shopping center (Gimbel's on corner) to Cheltenham Ave. Turn left at the next corner (Washington Lane), and proceed on Washington Lane to the third traffic light. Turn right on Ashbourne Rd. to the Retreat House* (6/10 *mile on the right).*

Pendle Hill
Wallingford, PA

A Quaker center for study and contemplation, Pendle Hill offers an opportunity to live in an educational community, attend classes, worship daily, and do cooperative work. It was founded in 1930 by members of the Religious Society of Friends and its philosophy comes from the four basic social testimonies of the Friends: equality of opportunity, simplicity of environment, harmony of inward and outward action, and community of daily interdependence of individuals and the spirit.

Pendle Hill is made up of 13 buildings on 22 acres in a suburban neighborhood outside Philadelphia. The quiet campus is planted with more than 140 different kinds of trees and shrubs that make it seem like a family compound. The community gathers in the dining room for three meals a day, sitting together at long tables. The food is served buffet-style and is delicious; there is often freshly baked bread and always attention to a balanced diet. The staff of 30 come from different professional backgrounds, and are highly qualified to present diverse courses in Quaker faith and practice, Bible studies, pottery, poetry, and weaving, as well as exploring one's vocation, looking to answer questions like What am I called to do now? How can I find the place to do it? and Who am I becoming?

There are rooms for 30 to 35 students who range in age from teenagers to youngsters of 75. The serious, committed students and staff demonstrate a spirit of fellowship that is apparent from the interplay at mealtime to the kitchen staff singing together as they clean up.

Each morning there is a meeting in silence, which may be broken by spoken ministry as the spirit moves those gathered together. The tradition is that ritual of service and place is unnecessary; one should live fully in the present, with truth and love.

One visitor observed that the spiritual should draw one into the world and be combined with regular life; people come here to develop spiritually and intellectually and take that to the home, office, and community. Even though "we often walk the lonesome valley by ourselves, we can learn to walk cheerfully over the earth, responding to the God in everyone. . . . Religion is not only a beatific vision, it is getting on with it."

Pendle Hill
338 ***Plush Mill Rd.***
Wallingford, PA *19086*
(215) 566-4507

Accommodations: *4 rooms for "sojourners," men and women, who can participate in resident programs from a few days to three weeks; guesthouses for groups can accommodate 30; 3 hermitages; fully catered and delicious vegetarian and nonvegetarian meals; kitchens in guesthouses if one wants to do one's own cooking; silent worship daily; 22 acres of lawn and woods; open year-round, though no guests are admitted for the last 2 weeks in August; $45 a night (rates are available for longer stays).*

Directions: *From the north, drive south from U.S. 1 on Rte. 252; from the south, take the Rte. 320 exit from I-95 at Chester and drive north on Rte. 252. Plush Mill Rd. is about 4/10 mile south of the Baltimore Pike off Rte. 252. The entrance to Pendle Hill is about 7/10 mile east on Plush Mill Rd.*

Rosemont Spiritual Center
Rosemont, PA

A former three-car garage behind Holy Child Convent has been converted into an unobtrusive but comfortable meeting place, a center for prayer, rest, and reflection. This triple-gabled stone building stands on the grounds of a former Main Line estate, and the original terraced lawns, garden fountains, and sculpture are still maintained.

The center, which is sponsored by the Society of the Holy Child Jesus, has rooms for six overnight guests, and the large meeting room in the basement can handle groups of 25. There is no formal retreat program, but the rooms are available for individuals seeking a quiet place, or for groups with their own spiritual purpose. The large living room is comfortably and tastefully furnished, and offers good reading places. There is a kitchen and dining area where guests prepare their own meals.

Rosemont College is just across the avenue, and daily mass is said there in the chapel. The lovely campus of this exclusive Catholic women's college is available for strolling. Just beyond the Rosemont campus is Villanova University, a relatively short walk or drive, where mass is also said daily.

Rosemont Spiritual Center
1359 ***Montgomery Ave.***
Rosemont, PA *19333*
(215) 527-4813

Accommodations: *6 rooms for men and women; kitchen for meal preparation; terraced gardens; near Rosemont and Villanova campuses; open year-round; $25 a night.*

Directions: *From I-76 (Schuylkill Expressway), take the Gulph Mills exit. (Coming from Valley Forge, the exit ramp leads directly into Montgomery Ave.; coming from Philadelphia, turn left at the end of exit ramp. This leads into Montgomery Ave.) When you see the* ROSEMONT COLLEGE *sign (about 3 miles from the expressway), move into left lane of traffic. Turn left into the first driveway after passing Wendover Ave., where a small white sign reads* HOLY CHILD CONVENT.

St. Joseph's-in-the-Hills Retreat House

Malvern, PA

Situated on 125 beautiful acres of woodlands, St. Joseph's-in-the-Hills is a complex of four dormitories, two chapels, two libraries, dining facilities, and a central auditorium. The main drive leads to the former manor house of the Coxe family, a substantial brick structure with a porch that overlooks a lawn over 100 yards long. This spacious home was used as the first retreat house.

In 1912 a Philadelphia businessman, John Ferreck, attended a lay retreat in New York City. On his return home he described the experience with such enthusiasm that he and his friends organized a retreat for themselves, formed a group called the Layman's Weekend Retreat League of Philadelphia, and eventually, in 1921, bought the Malvern property.

There is an interesting and unique concept here. The purpose of St. Joseph's is spiritual, yet the property and buildings are owned and maintained solely by laymen. The retreat center now has 17 full-time employees and 35 part-time. In the past year there were more than 20,000 attendees: 12,750 for weekend programs and 7,250 for midweek. The programs are Catholic-oriented but nondenominational in spirit. All are welcome—students and seniors, men and women, clergy and nuns. St. Joseph's accommodates and respects those who wish to make a private retreat. The costs are covered by a suggested contribution but no one is turned away for inability to pay.

Many groups and individuals have been attending regularly for years. One man who has come for 20 years said, "We're here basically for the same reason. We care about being good men." Another said, "What they give you here, you really can't go out and buy." Every year, hundreds of Philadelphia firemen and policemen come as a group, "for a chance to get away from the fray, a chance to meditate. By coming here you can be a better husband, father, policeman, or fireman."

Each room has a single bed, desk, and chair, with shared washrooms not far away. The two chapels are quiet places for reflection. The grounds surrounding the retreat complex have paths leading to four separate Ways of the Cross, so that even large groups are dispersed and each retreatant has a sense of privacy. One can wander for hours over the 125 acres and visit the many shrines, such as Our Lady of Grace and the Pietà. The detailed map in the centerfold of the retreat manual, given to each attendee, shows the entire layout.

St. Joseph's-in-the-Hills Retreat House
2nd and Warren Ave.
Malvern, PA *19355*
(215) 644-0400

Accommodations: *For men only (women can come on private retreats only during a women's retreat), 323 singles, with basins; healthful, simple meals in the large dining room; walking paths on 125 acres; open year-round; requested contribution: $65 a weekend.*

Directions: *From I-276 (Pennsylvania Turnpike), take the Valley Forge exit; or from I-76 (Schuylkill Expressway), take the Rte. 202 South exit. Proceed south on Rte. 202 to the Paoli exit (Rte. 252). Proceed on Rte. 252 South to U.S. 30. Take U.S. 30 West; at the third traffic light, turn left on Paoli Pike. (From this point, Malvern Retreat signs will direct you.) At the third traffic light, turn right on Warren Ave. and continue to the sign reading* ST. JOSEPH'S-IN-THE-HILLS.

St. Raphaela Mary Retreat House

Haverford, PA

This three-story stone mansion was built in a quiet suburban neighborhood of Philadelphia's Main Line in the early 20th century. Catholic nuns acquired it in 1957 and immediately started a retreat center that, in its first year, had 360 retreatants. They now receive 3,600 annually and are self-supporting. The nuns make their facilities available to any denomination or group seeking a quiet, restful place to concentrate in relaxed surroundings. Their service is hospitality, and they celebrate people's desire to be renewed and refreshed.

Major renovations were completed in 1989. The stunningly beautiful main rooms have a soothing and harmonious blend of colors and textures that invite tranquillity and reflect the vision of the community and architect Agnes Kan. Up to 70 persons can be accommodated in comfortable single and double rooms. New washrooms were added, as well as sinks in each room, new plumbing and electricity, and air conditioning.

The sisters are called Handmaids of the Sacred Heart of Jesus. Their order was founded in 1877 in Spain by Saint Raphaela Mary. Following the rule of Saint Ignatius Loyola, their main mission is to educate. Their schools for wealthy children support those for the poor. They were attracted to this property because of the nearby Catholic colleges, Rosemont and Villanova, which make it easier for community members to continue their education.

The grounds behind the house are spacious and well kept. Some 70 yards back is a grotto, a statue of Blessed Mary with a covering built by a group of young men who came for a retreat and donated their time and skill.

The resident community has morning and evening prayer sessions that retreatants are welcome to attend. The nuns have an obligation to sit before the Blessed Sacrament an hour a day, and this they perform according to their individual schedules. When asked if there were special prayers to say at this time, one nun replied: "Oh, no . . . I just look at Him and He looks at me."

St. Raphaela Mary Retreat House
616 Coopertown Rd.
Haverford, PA 19041
(215) 642-5715

Accommodations: *For men, women, and children, 50 beds in singles, doubles, and triples; community meals; daily mass and evening prayer; library; 8 acres; open year-round; $35 a night.*

Directions: *From Philadelphia, using City Line Ave., turn right on Haverford Rd. Proceed 3 miles and turn left on College Ave. (watch for the Retreat House sign on the right in less than a mile).*

From Delaware County, take Darby Rd. to Coopertown Rd. Turn right to College Ave., and continue until the Retreat House sign appears on the left.

Pennsylvania: Other Places

San Damiano Center, Our Lady of Angels Convent, **Aston,** PA 19014. (215) 459-4125

Kirkridge, **Bangor,** PA 18013. (215) 588-1793

Green Hills Methodist Camp, **Barree,** PA 16615. (814) 669-4212. Mailing address: 900 South Arlington Ave., Room 112, Harrisburg, PA 17109

St. Mary's House of Greater Solitude, Rte. 1, P.O. Box 276, **Bedford,** PA 15522

Fatima House, Rolling Hills Rd., **Bedminster,** PA 18910. (215) 795-2947

St. Francis Center for Renewal, 395 Bridle Path Rd., **Bethlehem,** PA 18017. (215) 866-5030

Ciotti Manor, P.O. Box 25, Herman Road, **Butler,** PA 16039. (412) 287-4794

Trinity Spiritual Center, 3609 Simpson Ferry Road, **Camp Hill,** PA 17011. (717) 761-7355

Spruce Lake Retreat, RD 1, P.O. Box 605, **Canadensis,** PA 18325. (717) 595-7505

St. Gabriel's Retreat House, 631 Griffin Pond Rd., **Clarks Summit,** PA 18411 (717) 586-2791

Precious Blood Spirituality Center, St. Joseph Convent, **Columbia,** PA 17512. (717) 285-4536

Gilmary Diocesan Center, Flaugherty Run Rd., **Coraopolis,** PA 15108. (412) 264-8400

Our Lady of the Sacred Heart Convent, 1500 Woodcrest Ave., **Coraopolis,** PA 15108. (412) 264-5140

Mercy Consultation Center, **Dallas,** PA 18612. (717) 675-2131

Fatima Renewal Center, 1000 Seminary Rd., **Dalton,** PA 18414. (717) 563-8500

Regina Mundi Priory, Waterloo and Fairfield Rds., **Devon,** PA 19333. (215) 688-5130

St. Francis Friary Retreat House, 3918 Chipman Rd., **Easton,** PA 18042. (215) 258-3053

Sisters of St. Ann, Mount St. Ann Retreat House, P.O. Box 328, **Ebensburg,** PA 15931. (814) 472-9354

Orthodox Monastery of the Transfiguration, RD 1, P.O. Box 184x, **Ellwood City,** PA 16117. (412) 758-4002

Ecclesia Center, 9109 Ridge Rd., **Gerard,** PA 16417. (814) 774-9691

Cardinal Wright Vocation and Prayer Center, Babcock Blvd., P.O. Box 252, RD 4, **Gibsonia,** PA 15044. (412) 961-6884

Lutheran Deaconess Community Center, 801 Merion Square Rd., **Gladwyne,** PA 19035. (215) 642-8838

Kirby Episcopal House, Sunset Rd., P.O. Box 370, **Glen Summit,** PA 18707. (717) 474-5800

St. Emma Retreat House, 1001 Harvey St., **Greensburg,** PA 15601. (412) 834-3060

Ciotti Manor, P.O. Box 25, Herman Rd., **Herman,** PA 16039. (412) 287-4749

Agape Ministries Bible Camp, RD 1, P.O. Box 64, **Hickory,** PA 15340. (412) 356-2308

The Himalayan Institute, RR 1, P.O. Box 400, **Honesdale,** PA 13431. (717) 253-5551

Camp Sequanota Enrichment Center, **Jennerstown,** PA 15547. (814) 629-6627

St. Vincent Summer Retreat House, **Latrobe,** PA 15650 (412) 539-9761

Mount Assisi Monastery, St. Francis Laymen's Retreat League, P.O. Box 38, **Loretto,** PA 15940. (814) 472-5324

Olmstead Manor Adult Retreat Renewal Center, P.O. Box 8, **Ludlow,** PA 16333. (814) 945-6512

Laurelville Mennonite Church Center, Rte. 5, P.O. Box 145, **Mount Pleasant,** PA 15666. (412) 423-2056

Villa of Our Lady Retreat House, HCR #1, P.O. Box 41, **Mount Pocono,** PA 18344. (717) 839-7217

Mount Asbury Methodist Center, RD 1, **Newville,** PA 17241. (717) 486-3827. Mailing address: 900 South Arlington Ave., Room 112, Harrisburg, PA 47109

St. Barnabas House Retreat and Conference Center, 12430 East Lake Rd., **North East,** PA 16428. (814) 725-4850

Fatima House, Rolling Hills Rd., **Ottsville,** PA 18942. (215) 795-2947

Medical Mission Sisters, 8400 Pine Rd., Fox Chase, **Philadelphia,** PA 19111 (215) 742-6100

St. Margaret's House, 5419 Germantown Ave., **Philadelphia,** PA 19144. (215) 844-9410

Carlow College Campus Ministry, 3333 Fifth Ave., **Pittsburgh,** PA 15213. (412) 578-6065

Cenacle Retreat House, 4721 Fifth Ave., **Pittsburgh,** PA 15213. (412) 681-6180

St. Paul's Retreat House, 148 Monastery Ave., **Pittsburgh,** PA 15203. (412) 381-7676

Fellowship Farm, RD 3, Saratoga Rd., **Pottstown,** PA 19464. (215) 326-3008

Annunciation House of Prayer, 1035 Evergreen Rd., **Reading,** PA 19611. (215) 372-8209

Precious Blood Convent, P.O. Box 97, **Shillington,** PA 19607. (215) 777-1624

Holy Shankaracharya Order, RD 3, P.O. Box 3430, **Stroudsburg,** PA 18360. (717) 629-0481

Mount St. Macrina Retreat Center, 510 West Main St., P.O. Box 878, **Uniontown,** PA 15401 (412) 437-1400

Villa Maria Community Center, **Villa Maria,** PA 16155. (412) 964-8861

Jesuit Center for Spiritual Growth, P.O. Box 223, Church Rd., **Wernersville,** PA 19565-0223. (215) 678-8085

Providence Center, Quarry Rd., **Yardley,** PA 19067. (215) 968-5464

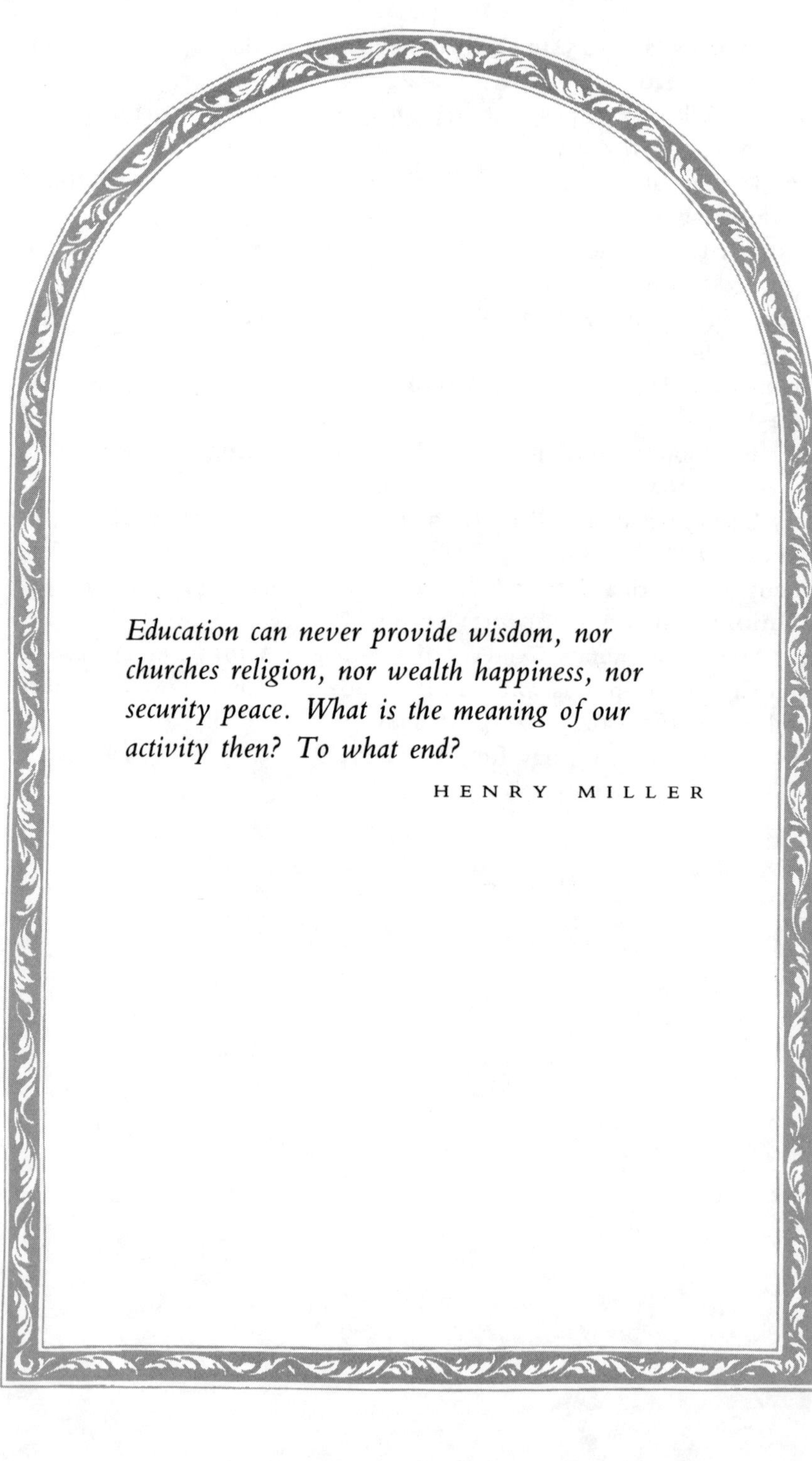

Education can never provide wisdom, nor churches religion, nor wealth happiness, nor security peace. What is the meaning of our activity then? To what end?

HENRY MILLER

Rhode Island

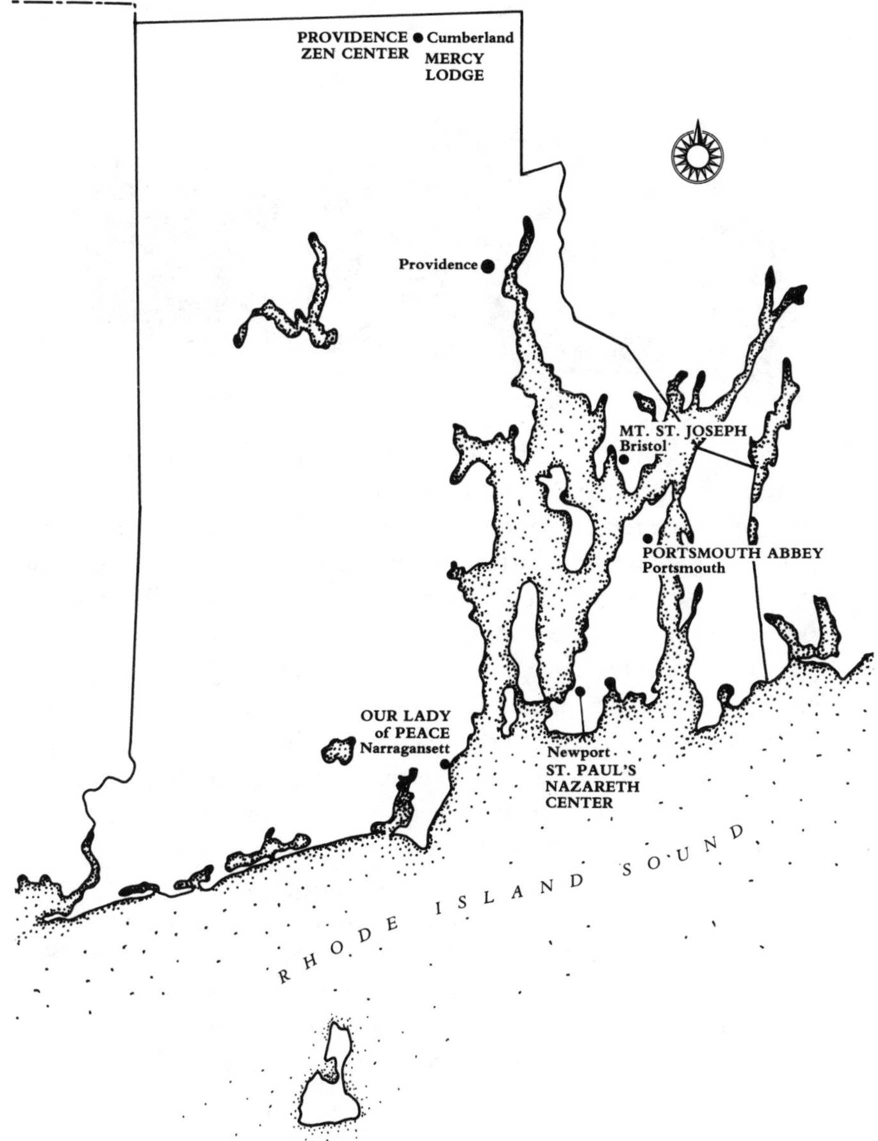

Mercy Lodge
Cumberland, RI

In the northwestern corner of Rhode Island, just a few miles from the Massachusetts border, Mercy Lodge sits on a hilltop up and away from road distractions, looking over nearby Lake Miscoe. This retreat house was built in 1912 as a hunting lodge, and the dark wood trim in the spacious rooms and the great fireplace still gives the feeling of a comfortable country home.

The lodge was used as a provincial house by the Sisters of Mercy from 1932, when they acquired it, until 1972, when they moved to a new brick building closer to the main road. Since then the lodge has become a house of prayer and a setting for the regular program of guided and directed retreats aimed at awakening spirituality and developing a greater understanding of the use of prayer in daily life. The nuns also offer a series of day and evening sessions, one a month for six months, on keeping a journal as a spiritual exercise. Called the Inigo (In-I-Go), this course is based on the teaching of Saint Ignatius Loyola. Through writing and music, Ignatius tells his story and leads one into the process of keeping a journal to recognize God at work in one's life. Private retreatants are accommodated, and the lodge is also available for prayer groups.

The kitchen is always open for snacks to supplement the home-cooked meals and the staff strives for a sense of hospitality and warmth. There is a sense of peacefulness and quiet purpose here in the clean, comfortable rooms, the many reading nooks, and the enclosed porch where one can sit and read or look out over the hills and valleys.

Only two miles away, in Wrentham, Massachusetts, is the Trappistine monastery of Mount St. Mary's Abbey (see page 60) where daily mass is celebrated.

Mercy Lodge
P.O. Box *7651*
Cumberland, RI *02864*
(401) 333-2801

Accommodations: *Singles and doubles for 13 men and women (can be extended to 24 by using the Watch Hill, Rhode Island, summer house on the coast); 3 home-cooked meals a day; community prayer daily; over 100 acres for hiking; Lake Miscoe adjoins the property; closed in summer; $30 a night, $70 a weekend; $80 a weekend at Watch Hill.*

Directions: *From I-95, take Exit 23 to Rte. 146 North. From Rte. 146, take I-295 North to Exit 11; turn left on Rte. 114 North to Rte. 121, and turn right onto Wrentham Rd. Pass the* MERCY MT. SCHOOL *sign and* ADMINISTRATION OFFICE TO MOUNT ST. RITA *sign; turn here to the top of the hill; watch for* MERCY LODGE *sign, and go left to the top of the next hill.*

Mount St. Joseph Spiritual Life Center

Bristol, RI

On 25 acres of woods and well-tended lawns, this retreat on Monkey Wrench Lane overlooks Mount Hope Bay and the Mount Hope Bay Bridge. Acquired in 1967 by the Catholic Sisters of St. Dorothy, the house was initially used for novices, then evolved into a home for the community. In 1986 the nuns began to share their peaceful and beautiful environment with individuals and groups needing a place in which to reflect and relax.

The sisters offer days of renewal, with themes relating to the church calendar, and retreats are scheduled throughout the year. There are 15 beds available in clean, well-kept rooms reached by a handsome polished wood staircase. Meals are served family-style in the kitchen or in the dining room. The large, enclosed front porch looking out to the bay is a wonderful place to sit and just rest.

The nuns come together to pray twice a day in the chapel, and sometimes one of them, an accomplished musician, plays the flute or guitar to accompany the service. A seven-minute walk back up Monkey Wrench Lane is a Catholic Columbian seminary where mass is celebrated daily at 8 A.M.

The nuns here have a strong sense of commitment, perhaps inherited from their founder, Paula Frassinetti, who, in the class-conscious society of Italy in the 19th century, opened a school for the poor each time she opened a school for the upper classes. The nuns made certain that the richer schools supported the poorer ones.

After Paula's death, people prayed for her help, and miracles began to occur. In 1930 she was beatified. But, as one nun pointed out, "to get to sainthood, we needed a big one!" In the early 1980s, prayers were offered for a devout woman who had been in bed for 13 years with paralyzed, misshapen legs. Nuns of St. Dorothy interceded with their foundress, the Blessed Paula. The crippled woman was instructed in a vision to keep praying and have faith, and a cure would take place. The woman did as she was told, and one day rose from her bed, completely cured. That was the "big one," and Paula Frassinetti was canonized in 1984.

Mount St. Joseph Spiritual Life Center
13 ***Monkey Wrench Lane***
Bristol, RI *02809*
(401) 253-5434 ***or*** *253-4630*

Accommodations: *For 13 men and women, 6 singles and doubles in the main house; 19 additional beds are available at Columbian Fathers Seminary, down the road; a 6-bedroom cottage on Narragansett Bay is available for rent in summer; home cooking is served in a casual dining room daily except Sunday; morning and evening prayer except Sunday; 11-mile bicycle path nearby (and bicycles are available); 15 acres; open year-round (no groups in July); $25 a night; cottage, $700 a week.*

Directions: *From Newport, take Rte. 114. After the Mount Hope Bridge, turn left (watch for the glass-enclosed bus stop) onto Low Lane. From there, follow the arrows indicating* ST. DOROTHY'S.

From Providence, take I-95 East to Exit 2 (Newport/Warren), then Rte. 136 South through Warren and Bristol. Turn right on Low Lane (last turn-off before Mount Hope Bridge) and proceed as above.

Nazareth Center
Newport, RI

This retreat house is right next to the famous Newport Cliff Walk, which can be reached by a path at the edge of the property. The two-story house has sweeping ocean views looking out over Easton Beach from a height of more than 50 feet. With its fireplace and comfortable furniture, it has the ambiance of a favorite aunt's beach house.

The Roman Catholic Sisters of St. Chrétienne bought the property in 1969 to house novitiates studying at nearby Salve Regina College. In 1984 they established a retreat center offering a program of directed retreats and workshops that include celebrating the single life, exploring dreams, understanding the Enneagram, and inquiring into how the saints experienced God in their daily lives. Those who wish to come for a private retreat are also welcome.

The community meets for Lauds at 7:30 A.M. and Vespers at 4:45 P.M. Guests and retreatants are welcome at these services, and there are several churches nearby where mass can be attended.

Breakfast and lunch are pick-up-style in the kitchen, which has a great view of the beginning of the Cliff Walk. The entire community meets for the evening meal, which is home-cooked, hearty, and delicious. There are nine beds for guests in four rooms with shared baths. Every bedroom has a view of the sea.

The open atmosphere encourages the neighbors to use the chapel, and the local Episcopalian minister often comes for a meal. Away from the hustle of the world, the center is an outpost of tranquillity at the edge of the sea.

Nazareth Center
12 Cliff Terrace
Newport, RI 02840
(401) 847-1654

Accommodations: *For men, women, and supervised children, 4 doubles and 1 single, all with ocean view; pick-up breakfast and lunch, community dinner, and Sunday brunch; Lauds and Vespers daily; located on the ocean at the beginning of the Cliff Walk; swimming pool; closed July and August; $25 a night.*

Directions: *From the north, take I-95 South; in Providence take I-195 East; in Fall River take Exit 8A to Rte. 24, which ends on Rte. 114. Stay on Rte. 114 until it meets Rte. 214 at a set of traffic lights (corner of Newport Furniture Store and Colonial Ice Cream). Turn left on Rte. 214; go to the end; take a right onto Memorial Blvd. (Easton Beach is on the left). After the Cliff Manor Restaurant, turn left onto Cliff Ave., then left again on Cliff Terrace. The center is the last house on the left.*

From the West, take I-95 North to Rte. 138 East to Newport; after the Newport Bridge, follow signs for downtown to America's Cup Blvd.; at the end, bear left at the lights onto Memorial Blvd., turn right onto Cliff Ave., then turn left onto Cliff Terrace. The center is the last house on the left.

Our Lady of Peace Spiritual Life Center

Narragansett, RI

This majestic mansion and its more than 70 acres of secluded woods are only a short walk from the rocky coastline. The Catholic-oriented center, which celebrated its fifteenth anniversary in 1989, offers an all-encompassing program designed to fit into family and business life.

Under the leadership of Sister Kiernan Flynn, an Irish nun who started her ministry by providing prisoners in Pawtucket with spiritual counseling, the group of nuns and laypeople now give 50 weekend retreats each year, and have a three-year Spirituality of Christian Leadership Program that blends psychological and theological studies with spirituality. One retired public-school superintendent who graduated from the program was asked what it felt like, having been "somebody" for so long, now to be nobody? He replied, "No, not true. It is now that I realize I am somebody."

The center has accommodations for 52 people in single rooms with communal washrooms. Meals are taken in a large dining room with a separate table for those observing silence. The retreat rooms are in a wing attached to the house where the staff lives. There are meeting and conference rooms for small and large groups, and a chapel and a prayer-meditation room at the base of the stone tower named Burning Bush. Apart from the mansion, there are four hermitages.

There is an old barn behind the main building where retreat groups of eight or nine study crafts such as pottery, weaving, drawing, dance, dialogue, and photography—a blend of focused activity to find the spirit within. The grounds around the buildings are beautifully kept, and there is a small pond with outdoor Stations of the Cross around it.

Our Lady of Peace Spiritual Life Center
Box 507, Ocean Rd.
***Narragansett, RI** 02882*
*(401) 783-2871 **or** 884-7676*

Accommodations: *For men and women, 52 singles with sinks, and 4 hermitage apartments; tasty cafeteria-style dining; 70+ acres, ocean and beach 1 block away; closed Christmas and New Year's; $35 a night.*

Directions: *From the north, take I-95 to Exit 9, then Rte. 4 South to Rte. 1. Exit from Rte. 1 at Point Judith/Scarborough. Turn right at the exit and cross Rte. 1, straight through the traffic light to South Pier Rd. Follow South Pier Rd. to the end, at Ocean Rd. Turn right onto Ocean Rd. Our Lady of Peace is 1/2 mile on the right.*

From the south, take I-95 to Connecticut Exit 92 (Stonington/Pawcatuck). Turn right and follow Rte. 2 East about 1 1/2 miles to Rte. 78. Turn right onto Rte. 78 and proceed to its end at U.S. 1. Turn left onto U.S. 1. Go about 20 miles to the Narragansett/Point Judith/Scarborough exit. Turn right at the top of the ramp, and cross the traffic light to South Pier Rd. Follow South Pier Rd. to its end at Ocean Rd. Turn right onto Ocean Rd. Our Lady of Peace is 1/2 mile on the right.

Portsmouth Abbey
Portsmouth, RI

Portsmouth Abbey is a community of Benedictine monks, located on 500 acres of shorefront on Narragansett Bay. The monastery, just seven miles north of Newport, was founded in 1918. Following the English Benedictine tradition, in 1926 the monks opened a college-prep school for boys modeled on the British boarding-school system, with the aim of educating bright young Catholics to enter the non-Catholic world as intellectual equals. The school has grown from a student body of 20 to its current number of more than 240 boys, 88 percent of whom are Catholic. All the boys go on to college.

There are four single rooms available for male guests. Meals are taken with the monks. There is also a small house where couples can stay. During the summer, group retreats are held for up to 80 people using the boys' dormitory and cafeteria.

This is one of the most traditional of the Benedictine communities in the United States. The monks still observe the rule of requesting permission from the abbot before they leave the property; they also observe the Chapter of Faults, every Wednesday evening, when monks acknowledge before the community any transgression of monastery rules.

The monks sing the canonical hours beginning at 5:45 A.M., and assemble six times a day in the magnificent stone and wood chapel.

The church is octagonal, with a tall spire. Inside there is seating for several hundred arranged in tiers that slope gently to the central altar, above which a gold crucifix, designed by a Jewish sculptor, is suspended from a multitude of fine wires radiating out like beams of light. The solemnity and power of the liturgy seem to take on a new dimension in such a dramatic setting.

Even when school is in session, this is a good place for reflective time: the lovely chapel, the example of the monks' prayerful life, and the spacious grounds to wander in.

To celebrate the graduation of his son, American artist Harry Jackson donated a sculpture that is in the main lobby. The bronze statue, a cowboy on horseback swinging a lariat, is inscribed with the words, "When you rope a dream, tie hard 'n fast 'n never turn it loose."

Portsmouth Abbey
Portsmouth, RI *02871*
(401) 683-2000

Accommodations: *A small guesthouse for couples, and a few rooms for men and friends of the abbey in the monastery, during school year; in summer the abbey can accommodate retreats of up to 80 people; tasty meals in the cafeteria or with the monks; sung prayer services and mass daily in a stunning chapel; 500 acres overlooking Narragansett Bay; all sports facilities; open year-round; $45 a night.*

Directions: *From I-95, take Exit 3 to Rte. 138 East. Follow signs to Jamestown and Newport bridges; take the second exit after Newport Bridge (Admiral Kalbfus Rd.). Turn left off the exit, and left again at the second stoplight (Rte. 114). After nine miles on Rte. 114, a green highway sign will appear on the right,* PORTSMOUTH ABBEY. *Turn left onto Cory's Lane, and drive one mile to the school entrance, on the right.*

Providence Zen Center

Cumberland, RI

The stone wall that borders the property and the imposing oriental gate at the main entrance give a sense of timelessness, as though the Providence Zen Center had been here for hundreds of years. In fact, the center was founded in 1972 by Seung Sahn, the first Korean Zen master to live and teach in the West. In 1979 the center acquired this former Seventh-Day Adventist nursing home. Only 15 miles from downtown Providence, the 50 wooded acres are in a quiet, remote setting.

The main building has been modified over the years to suggest a Zen temple, and there is a gong or temple bell in one corner of the property. Behind and above the main building, in a grove of trees, is the Diamond Hill Zen Monastery, used as a residence for monks and for long retreats. This is a classic Japanese structure, both inside and out, built for the most part by Zen Center students.

As you enter the main building, you take off your shoes and change to the slippers provided or simply wear your socks—an oriental custom so sensible that it may never be adopted in the West. The facilities in this rambling building include two large meditation halls, a kitchen, a dining room where meals are taken sitting on pillows in a circle, and a library and reading room.

There are morning and evening chanting and meditation periods.

The beautiful wood floors of the meditation hall have sitting pillows arranged in a neat, U pattern around a Buddha statue and altar.

There is a full program of retreats ranging from one day to a weekend, and the 90-day summer and winter *Kyol Che* ("coming together"), which students can take in segments of two weeks or longer.

The practice of Zen enables the individual to let go of those habits of the mind that cause sorrow—ideas, opinions, judgments—to perceive this moment more clearly. As one learns to live in a simple, nonclinging way, one becomes enriched and nourished and this helps one treat others more compassionately.

The reply to the query, Why go on a retreat? is answered in direct Zen style: A retreat is an opportunity to cultivate silence within yourself, eat simple food with gratitude, work with mindfulness, sit with your heart, and sleep. You suspend ideas of past, future, and present and ask yourself, "How is it *just now?*"

Providence Zen Center
528 Pound Rd.
Cumberland, RI 02864
(401) 658-1464 (9 A.M.–noon and 1–4 P.M., Mon.–Fri.)

Accommodations: *9 private rooms at the center, plus groups in the meditation room; camping, plus rooms in adjoining Diamond Hill Zen Monastery for men, women, and children; vegetarian meals made by rotating cooks; daily morning and evening meditation, and work; 50 wooded acres, pond for swimming or ice skating; a variety of retreats, including guest weekends to introduce people to Zen; open year-round; guest weekends $50.*

Directions: *Providence Zen Center is located 15 miles north of Providence. From I-295, take Exit 10 (Rte. 122, Mendon Rd.) At the traffic light at the end of the ramp, turn right and go north 1 1/2 miles on Mendon Rd. After you pass under the footbridge, take the next right onto Pound Rd. (If you pass a Gulf station, you have gone too far on Mendon Rd.) Drive 3/4 mile on Pound Rd. Providence Zen Center is on the right.*

St. Paul's Priory Guest House

Newport, RI

A ten-foot-high wall surrounds this three-and-one-half-acre estate in a neighborhood of grand Newport mansions. The property was acquired in 1962 by the Roman Catholic Sisters of Jesus Christ Crucified. In 1930, Mother Marie des Douleurs established this French order of contemplative nuns in order to provide a sanctuary for sick, infirm, and handicapped women who wanted to live a religious life but were not readily accepted in other orders. The sisters follow the Benedictine tradition: a dedication to silence, prayer, simple enclosure, and celebration of the canonical hours.

The nuns meet six times a day in the large, high-ceilinged chapel, which has pews for a few dozen guests. The liturgy is often accompanied on the organ by one of the nuns. The peace and joy radiating from these dedicated women is almost palpable.

Guests stay in a converted stable on the property. There is room for six year-round, nine in summer. The rooms are cozy and quiet, and there is a community kitchen stocked with basics. If they wish, guests may take the noon meal around a large table with the sisters in the mansion.

This elegant neighborhood has one huge mansion after another. Salve Regina College is ten minutes away, near the famous Cliff Walk. There one can walk for hours above the ocean breaking on the rocks below.

Retreatants appreciate the quiet and the opportunity to join the nuns in their daily liturgy. The peace, contentment, and charity they embody benefits all who give it, receive it, and see it.

As one nun said, "No handicap is an obstacle to helping others spiritually, intellectually, emotionally, and materially, even financially, by skills or professional work. The Chinese character for *man* looks as though it is one man supporting another. This is reality for me."

St. Paul's Priory Guest House
61 Narragansett Ave.
Newport, RI 02840
(401) 847-2423

Accommodations: *Men, women, and children in 2 doubles and 2 singles, plus an apartment on the main floor in the summer, in this former stable; well-stocked kitchen (you can join the community for the noon meal in the priory if you are on retreat); prayer 4 times daily; 2 blocks from ocean and Cliff Walk; open year-round; free-will offering.*

Directions: *From Rte. 95, take Exit 3 East to Rte. 138 East. Follow signs to Jamestown and Newport bridges. Turn right onto Farewell St.; at the second traffic light, take a right onto America's Cup Ave. Stay in the left lane, which turns up Memorial Blvd.; at the first traffic light, turn right onto Bellevue and proceed to Narragansett Ave. Turn right. The priory is the first house on the left, with a small sign on the wall; ring the bell.*

Rhode Island: Other Places

St. Dominic Savio Youth Center, 211A Broadrock Rd., **Peacedale,** RI 02883. (401) 783-4055

Father Marot CYO Center, 53 Federal St., **Woonsocket,** RI 02895. (401) 762-3252

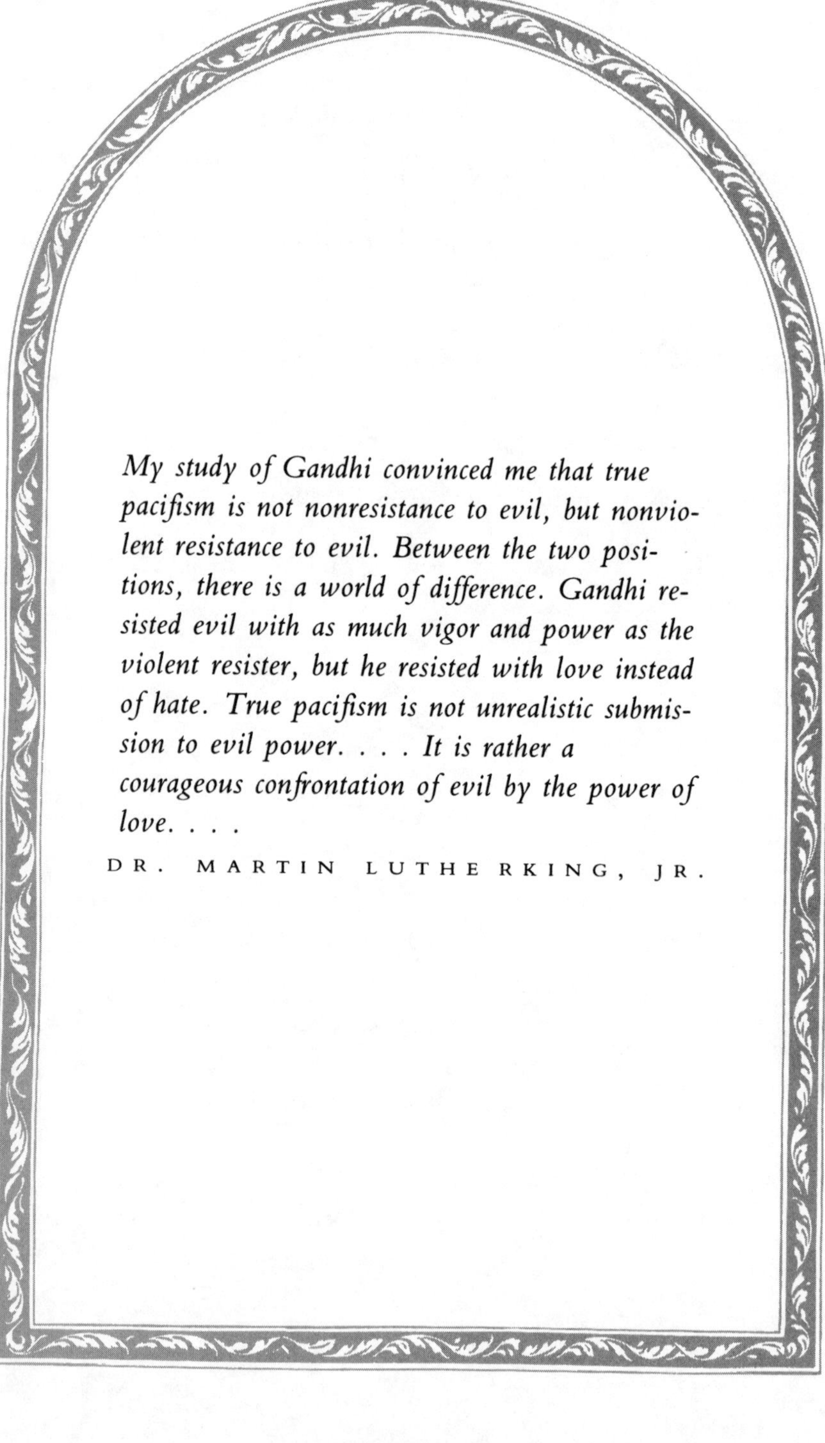

My study of Gandhi convinced me that true pacifism is not nonresistance to evil, but nonviolent resistance to evil. Between the two positions, there is a world of difference. Gandhi resisted evil with as much vigor and power as the violent resister, but he resisted with love instead of hate. True pacifism is not unrealistic submission to evil power. . . . It is rather a courageous confrontation of evil by the power of love. . . .

DR. MARTIN LUTHER KING, JR.

Vermont

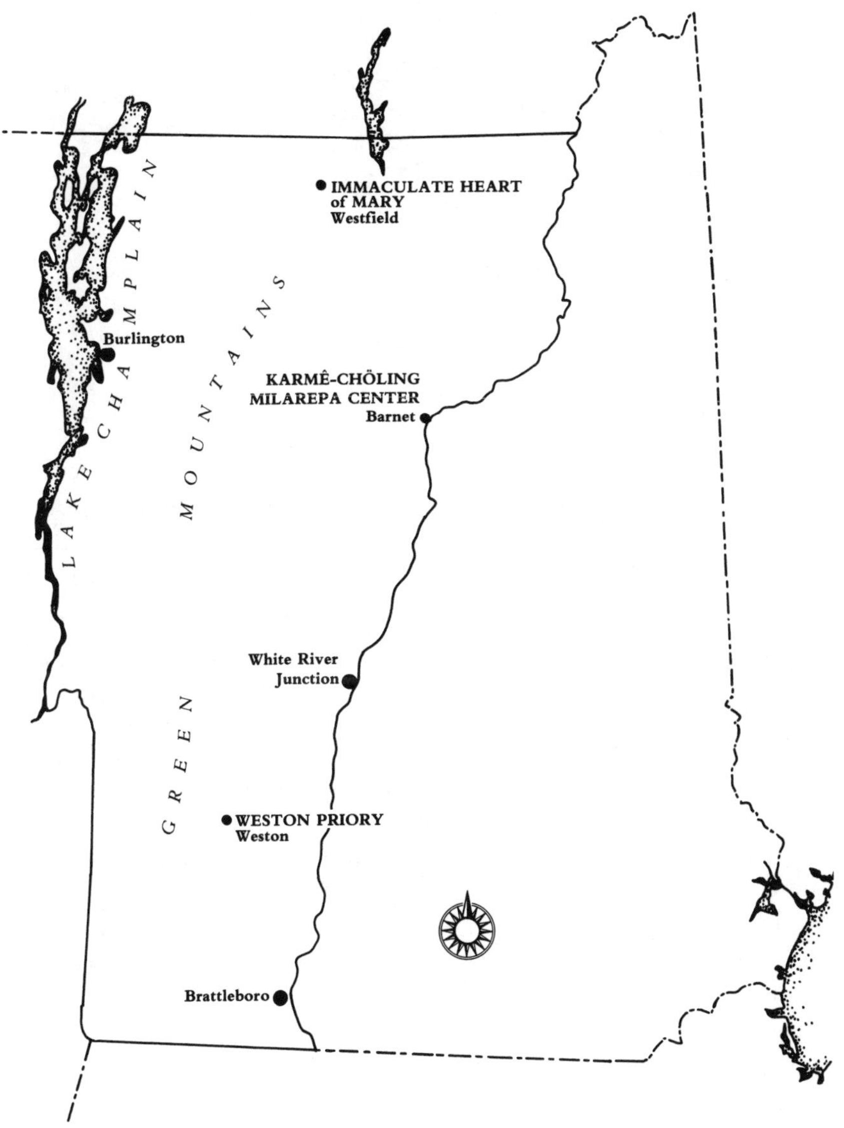

LAKE CHAMPLAIN
GREEN MOUNTAINS
IMMACULATE HEART of MARY
Westfield
Burlington
KARMÊ-CHÖLING MILAREPA CENTER
Barnet
White River Junction
WESTON PRIORY
Weston
Brattleboro

Karmê-Chöling

Barnet, VT

About one hour north of White River Junction in northern Vermont, just outside the town of Barnet, is Karmê-Chöling (Tail of the Tiger), a Tibetan Buddhist meditation and retreat center. Founded in the early 1970s by the late Chögyam Trungpa, Rimpoche, this was one of the first *vajrayana* centers outside of India. Guidance is offered in meditation practice, the study of Buddhist philosophy and psychology, and the application of these teachings in daily life.

The center is on 540 acres of wooded country. As you approach, you look across a pond to buildings with an unmistakable Tibetan design—one of which is emblazoned with a large red and gold circle. The main buildings house the staff, a large dining room where meals are taken cafeteria-style, plus the sitting hall, conference rooms, guest rooms, and private meditation rooms.

There are many levels of meditation practice available: introductory weekends for those with little or no experience; the *dathun* or one-month group meditation retreat; Shambhala training; and in-house or residence retreats where visitors may come for any length of time and follow the daily schedule of five hours of meditation and three and a half hours of work, plus evening classes. This has the benefit of group support and close contact with a meditation instructor. There are also hermitage retreats where individuals may practice alone in a cabin in the woods for ten days or more. Meals are taken to them, and the areas are marked to ensure privacy.

There are many levels of accommodation, from private to semi-private rooms, cabins, tents or a sleep-in tent dormitory, or the shrine room floor. The center also owns a charming hotel in the town of Barnet, usually used for groups.

This is a bustling, well-organized and well-managed school that can deal with large numbers of students and practitioners. Childcare is available for children two years of age and older, at a moderate charge. There is plenty of space to wander on the property, especially for the conditioned hiker. From the main buildings a dirt road winds up the hill with small shrines along the way, past the concealed hermitages to an open field where there is a large outdoor shrine. Convocations are held here in the summer, and hundreds gather for special events.

Karmê-Chöling
Barnet, VT *05821*
(802) 633-2384 (1–6 P.M.)

Accommodations: *Well over 100 men, women, and children can be housed in a variety of private, semiprivate, cabin, tent and shrine-room accommodations, plus a small hotel in town; delicious vegetarian and non-vegetarian food in cafeteria-style dining room; daily meditation; work periods required; 540 acres; open year-round; rates from $25 a night for private room and work to free tent, dorm, or shrine-room accommodations in exchange for work; there is also a daily retreat cost; free meditation instruction; childcare is sometimes available.*

Directions: *Located in northern Vermont, one hour north of White River Junction, 1/2 mile west of Exit 18 on I-91.*

Milarepa Center
Barnet, VT

Up a steep drive and past the famous "Monk Crossing" road sign, this 270-acre farm adjacent to Karmê-Chöling is named after an 11th-century Tibetan monk, poet, and spiritual teacher. Milarepa's life was a testament to the discipline of achieving liberation through the Buddhist system of mental development. He was a perplexing figure to the people of Tibet, yet he became both a saint and a folk hero whose universal teaching is still relevant today. As described in the book *Miraculous Journey,* translated by Lama Kunga Rimpoche and Brian Cutillo (Lotsawa, 1986), Milarepa, "playing the wandering, homeless stranger . . . made the only trip he considered worthwhile—to the natural state of mind, where one is in harmony with all beings and things."

Milarepa is one of 30 Buddhist centers belonging to the Foundation for the Preservation of the Mahayana Tradition (FPMT), an international network of Buddhist communities founded in 1971. The aim of FPMT is to make Buddhist philosophy and teachings available in the most appropriate form in each part of the world.

The 12-room farmhouse has a large kitchen, staff living rooms, very simple communal guest rooms, and a meditation room. There is also a garage and barn. Guests should bring their own bedding and be prepared to help with cooking, cleaning, and all the tasks needed for a growing community. Visitors are welcome at any time except during winter retreats from December to March.

The center runs regular retreats for the rest of the year, some oriented to family participation. Guest facilities are limited, so camping is encouraged. For those seekers who appreciate the rusticity of northern Vermont, with its mild summers and cool springs and autumns, the setting is quiet and peaceful.

Milarepa Center
Barnet Mountain
***Barnet, VT** 05821*
(802) 633-4136

Accommodations: *2 simple dormitory rooms with mattresses, plus camping facilities in summer on this 270-acre farm; community meals; meditation, study, and work is the daily resident routine; open to visitors year-round except during December–March winter retreats; bring bedding; donations requested for rooms.*

Directions: *From north or south, take I-91 to Exit 18. Go east to Barnet, then take U.S. 5 North 1/2 mile from the general store to a steep drive on left. From east or west, take U.S. 2 to St. Johnsbury, then proceed south on U.S. 5 about 8 miles to the drive, which is on the right.*

Monastery of the Immaculate Heart of Mary

Westfield, VT

In northern Vermont, less than an hour from the Canadian border, a congregation of Solesmes nuns—a contemplative order following the Rule of St. Benedict—have found an ideal setting for their life of prayer and work. Some years ago a Canadian bought 400 acres of land on which to build a children's camp. It never materialized, however, so he donated the land to the local Catholic diocese. In the late 1970s, when the Solesmes of Quebec were looking for a site for a monastery, the diocesan bishop offered this land, and with the financial support of Canadians alone, the Monastery of the Immaculate Heart of Mary was built in 1981.

The monastery looks as though it were constructed only yesterday. The long, winding driveway is bordered with newly planted trees, and the complex has a fresh look, its bricks red and clean.

The gift shop carries postcards with watercolor scenes of the monastery by the resident chaplain, Father Guy Marie Oury. An experienced spiritual counselor and painter, he has also written 40 books dealing with monasticism and early Christianity in Canada. Born in France, he entered the Benedictine order in Tours in 1947. He was assigned to Westfield, a perfect place to write and paint.

There are seven guest rooms in one wing for women retreatants.

Meals are taken alone or with other guests. The nuns meet eight times a day, from 6:30 A.M. to 8:40 P.M., in the L-shaped chapel, to observe the canonical hours. The altar is at the corner of the L, one wing for the nuns who take their places in the stalls, behind an iron grate, signifying their separateness from the world. Their singing is pure joy. The chaplain celebrates high mass in Latin at 9:45 A.M. Walking down the wide, silent corridors to the chapel gives the feeling of being in a medieval monastery. This place provides a real experience for women who would like to sample contemplative monastic life.

Monastery of the Immaculate Heart of Mary
HCR Box 11
Westfield, VT 05874
(802) 744-6525

Accommodations: *For women only, a 4-bedroom guesthouse adjoining the monastery; private dining room; 7 offices daily plus mass; 400 acres; open year-round; $20 a night.*

Directions: *Located in northern Vermont. Take I-91 North to the Orleans exit, then Rte. 58 West (of which a 4–5 mile stretch is unpaved) to Rte. 100 North at Lowell. The monastery is on the right after about 4 miles.*

Weston Priory
Weston, VT

Weston Priory, a community of Benedictine monks, is located at the edge of the Green Mountain National Forest, four miles north of Weston. It was founded in 1953 by a brother from Dormition Abbey in Jerusalem, and other brothers have come from all parts of the United States, Canada, and Latin America. The many recordings of the monastery's extraordinary choir are sold as a means of financial support and a way to share the joy of community spirit. The monks also create woodcrafts and greeting cards and have a gallery of high-quality thematic pieces that demonstrate their social conscience. In 1984 the monastery was declared a public sanctuary for Central American refugees. The monks have given sanctuary to one Guatemalan family for five years. Since 1986 they have hosted an annual Festival of Solidarity, an interracial, intercultural gathering.

Down a quiet, tree-lined road are three guesthouses, each accommodating from three to six adults. These beautifully furnished cabins are set off from one another only a few minutes' walk from the chapel. Guests bring their own food and prepare it in the kitchen of their guesthouse. Utensils and linens are provided, and guests take care of their own cleaning. Individual men stay in the priory guesthouse; single women stay in a separate building called Morningside. These guests take their meals with the monks.

Retreatants are expected to plan their own time. There are regular daily services at the chapel beginning at 5 or 6 A.M. morning vigils, then either two or three midday prayer services, ending with Compline around 8 P.M. The modern orientation of the services makes them very popular. The monks are available by arrangement for informal discussions on specific topics such as community life or social justice.

The monastery is deep in the Green Mountains, offering an opportunity to explore the woodlands and follow the nature trails that the monks maintain. The monastery grounds are tended meticulously.

The Weston community has established a joint retreat effort with a community of Mexican Benedictine sisters in Cuernavaca, Mexico. Retreatants can go for ten days at a reasonable cost to experience the historical and cultural context of Mexican life, under the care and direction of Mexican nuns who actively work with the poor. The Weston brothers have also just helped open House of Sabbath, a retreat house in nearby Weston, to serve the poor, the homeless, and those working with them.

Weston Priory
RR *1*, ***Box*** *50*
Weston, VT *05161*
(802) 824-5409

Accommodations: *Up to 18 men and women can be accommodated in 3 guesthouses with kitchens, plus private rooms for 5 or 6 men at Priory Guest House, and 5 women in Morningside (meals taken with the brothers); ordinary length of stay at the priory is from 3 days to one week; common prayer 4–5 times daily, and Eucharist 5 times a week; 500 acres adjoining Green Mountain National Forest; closed 2 weeks following Labor Day, 2 weeks in June, and during occasional community retreats in January and February; free-will offering.*

Directions: *North on Rte. 100 to Rte. 155 for 1/4 mile. First left to priory. From Rockingham, take I-91 North. Take Exit 6 and go north on Rte. 103. Then take Rte. 11 West to Rte. 100 North. Continue on Rte. 100N to Weston, then after 3 1/2 miles take Rte. 155 for 1/4 mile. First left is the priory.*

Bishop Booth Conference Center, Rock Point, **Burlington,** VT 05401. (802) 658-6233

Mount St. Mary Convent, 100 Mansfield Ave., **Burlington,** VT 05401. (802) 863-6835

Mandala Buddhist Center, Quaker St., **Lincoln,** VT 05467. (802) 453-5038

Self-Realization Fellowship, Rte. 1, Box 519, **Shaftesbury,** VT 05257. (802) 442-4311

Glossary

Canonical hours The liturgy of the hours is the official daily prayer cycle of the Catholic Church, an adaptation of the liturgy of the synagogue, which has evolved over the centuries. The "hours" consist of Matins, Lauds, Terce, Sext, None, Vespers, and Compline. "Seven times a day I praise thee. . . ." (Psalms 119:164).

Centering prayer Meditative prayer, using a sacred word to focus attention internally. Father Thomas Keating's book *Open Mind, Open Heart* describes this in detail.

Charismatic retreat Christian healing retreat involving prophecy and praying in tongues.

Directed Retreat Usually a six-to-eight-day period of silent prayer that includes a daily meeting with a spiritual director.

Enneagram An ancient, nine-pointed circular diagram that can be used to identify personality types, bring insight into the divine activity within each person, and comprehend the organization of the universe.

Guided retreat Retreat that includes meeting with a spiritual director from time to time, but not on a daily basis.

Private Retreat A time of solitude without guidance or direction.

Rule of Saint Benedict Written in the 6th century by Saint Benedict, this code covers all aspects of monastic life and serves as a guide for the whole of Western monasticism. It emphasizes poverty, humility, and obedience, and its motto is "Work and prayer."

Shambhala The name of a mythical enlightened kingdom in ancient

Tibet. *The Sacred Path of the Warrior* by Chögyam Trungpa describes Shambhala practice, which is founded on the gentleness of the Buddhist tradition and directly cultivates who and what we are as human beings. A secular rather than a religious outlook for anyone seeking a genuine and fearless existence.

Sufism A school of Islamic mysticism that has grown to encompass many traditions and includes an elaborate symbolism much used by Islamic poets. There is scholarly disagreement on the exact origins of the name, some saying it comes from an Arabic translation of the Greek *sophia,* meaning "wisdom," others that it comes from the word *sūf* (wool) because of the coarse robes worn by early Sufi ascetics and renunciates. The contemporary Sufi Hazrat Inayat Khan taught that it is derived from the Arabic *saf* (pure).

Vajrayana The "diamond path," the Tantric school of Tibetan Buddhism.

Zazen Zen sitting meditation.

Zendo Room or hall used for the practice of zazen.

Featured Places

Abba House of Prayer, Albany, NY, 112–113
Abbey of Regina Laudis, Bethlehem, CT, 4–5
Abbey of the Genesee, Piffard, NY, 114–115
Abode of the Message, New Lebanon, NY, 116–117
Aryaloka, Newmarket, NH, 76–77
Bay View Villa, Saco, ME, 26–27
Benedictine Grange, West Redding, CT, 6–7
The Chaleight, Wells, NY, 118–119
Chapel House, Hamilton, NY, 120–121
Chautauqua Institution, Chautauqua, NY, 122–123
China Lake Conference Center, China, ME, 28–29
Chrysalis House, Warwick, NY, 124–125
The Common, Peterborough, NH, 78–79
Cormaria Center, Sag Harbor, NY, 126–127
Dai Bosatsu Zendo, Livingston Manor, NY, 128–129
Daylesford Abbey, Paoli, PA, 186–187
Dominican Retreat House, Elkins Park, PA, 188–189
Durham Retreat Center, Durham, NH, 80–81
Eastern Point Retreat House, Gloucester, MA, 46–47
Emery House, West Newbury, MA, 48–49
Ferry Beach, Saco, ME, 30–31
Glastonbury Abbey, Hingham, MA, 50–51
Good Shepherd Center, Morristown, NJ, 94–95
Goose Cove Lodge, Sunset, ME, 32–33
Graymoor, Garrison, NY, 154–155
Hersey Retreat, Stockton Springs, ME, 34–35
Holy Cross Monastery, West Park, NY, 130–131
Holy Trinity Community, Hornell, NY, 132–133
House of the Redeemer, New York, NY, 134–135
Hundred Acres Monastery, New Boston, NH, 82–83
Insight Meditation Society, Barre, MA, 52–53
Jesuit Retreat House, Auriesville, NY, 136–137
Karmê-Chöling, Barnet, VT, 222–223
Kripalu Center for Yoga and Health, Lenox, MA, 54–55
Linwood Spiritual Center, Rhinebeck, NY, 138–139
Loyola House of Retreats, Morristown, NJ, 96–97

Manchester Priory, Manchester, NH, 84–85
Marian Shrine, West Haverstraw, NY, 140–141
Marie Joseph Spiritual Center, Biddeford, ME, 36–37
Mercy Center, Madison, CT, 8–9
Mercy Lodge, Cumberland, RI, 204–205
Milarepa Center, Barnet, VT, 224–225
Miramar Retreat Center, Duxbury, MA, 56–57
Monastery of the Immaculate Heart of Mary, Westfield, VT, 226–227
Montfort Retreat Center, Litchfield, CT, 10–11
Mount Carmel Retreat House, Williamstown, MA, 58–59
Mount Irenaeus Franciscan Mountain Retreat, West Clarksville, NY, 142–143
Mount St. Alphonsus Spiritcare Center, Esopus, NY, 144–145
Mount St. Francis Hermitage, Maine, NY, 146–147
Mount St. Joseph Spiritual Life Center, Bristol, RI, 206–207
Mount St. Mary's Abbey, Wrentham, MA, 60–61
Mount Saviour Monastery, Pine City, NY, 148–149
Nazareth Center, Newport, RI, 208–209
New Skete Communities, Cambridge, NY, 150–151
Notre Dame Spiritual Center, Alfred, ME, 38–39
Oratory of the Little Way, Gaylordsville, CT, 12–13
Our Lady of Peace Spiritual Life Center, Narragansett, RI, 210–211
Our Lady of the Resurrection Monastery, La Grangeville, NY, 152–153
Our Lady's Guest and Retreat House, Garrison, NY, 154–155
Pendle Hill, Wallingford, PA, 190–191
Portsmouth Abbey, Portsmouth, RI, 212–213
The Priory, Chestertown, NY, 156–157
Providence Zen Center, Cumberland, RI, 214–215
Queen of Peace Retreat House, Newton, NJ, 102–103
Rosemont Spiritual Center, Rosemont, PA, 192–193
Sacred Heart Retreat House, Ipswich, MA, 62–63
St. Anselm Abbey, Manchester, NH, 84–85
St. Benedict Priory, Still River, MA, 64–65
St. Cuthbert's Retreat House, Brewster, NY, 158–159
St. Francis Center, Oyster Bay, NY, 160–161
St. Francis Retreat Center, Rye Beach, NH, 86–87
St. Gabriel's Retreat House, Shelter Island, NY, 162–163
St. Joseph-by-the-Sea, Peaks Island, ME, 40–41
St. Joseph's Abbey, Spencer, MA, 66–67
St. Joseph's-in-the-Hills, Malvern, PA, 194–195
St. Joseph Spiritual Life Center, Valatie, NY, 164–165
St. Marguerite's Retreat House, Mendham, NJ, 98–99
St. Mark's House of Prayer, Sag Harbor, NY, 126–127
St. Mary's Abbey-Delbarton, Morristown, NJ, 100–101
St. Mary's Villa, Sloatsburg, NY, 166–167
St. Paul's Abbey, Newton, NJ, 102–103
St. Paul's Priory Guest House, Newport, RI, 216–217
St. Raphaela Mary Retreat House, Haverford, PA, 196–197
St. Stephen Priory Spiritual Life Center, Dover, MA, 68–69
Springwater Center, Springwater, NY, 168–169
Star Island, Isle of Shoals, NH, 88–89
Still Point House of Prayer, Stillwater, NY, 170–171
Transfiguration Monastery, Windsor, NY, 172–173
Vikingsborg Guest House, Darien, CT, 14–15

Villa Maria Retreat House, Stamford, CT, 16–17
Villa Pauline, Mendham, NJ, 104–105
Visitation Center, Ridgefield, CT, 18–19
Wellsprings, Glens Falls, NY, 174–175
Weston Priory, Weston, VT, 228–229
Wisdom House, Litchfield, CT, 20–21
Zen Mountain Monastery, Mount Tremper, NY, 176–177

Other Places

Adelynrood, Byfield, MA, 71
Agape Ministries Bible Camp, Hickory, PA, 200
Aldersgate Center, Swartswood, NJ, 108
Ananda Ashram, Monroe, NY, 181
Annunciation House of Prayer, Reading, PA, 201
Archdiocesan Spirit Life Center, Bloomfield, CT, 23
Arrowood, Rye Brook, NY, 182
Barlin Acres, Boylston, MA, 71
Barry House, Brant Lake, NY, 179
Beaver Cross Camp, Springfield Center, NY, 182
Beaver Conference Farm, Yorktown Heights, NY, 183
Beaver Camp, Lowville, NY, 180
Bellinger Hall, Chautauqua Institution, Chautauqua, NY, 179
Bement Camp and Conference Center, Charlton Depot, MA, 71
Bethany House, Syracuse, NY, 182
Bethany Retreat House, Highland Mills, NY, 180
Bethlehem Hermitage, Chester, NJ, 107
Bishop Booth Conference Center, Burlington, VT, 231
Bishop Molloy Passionist Retreat House, Jamaica Estates, NY, 180
Briarwood Conference Center, Monument Beach, MA, 72
Cabrini-on-the-Hudson, West Park, NY, 183
Calvary Retreat Center, Shrewsbury, MA, 72
Camp Ma-He-Tu, Bear Mountain, NY, 179
Camp Blairhaven, South Duxbury, MA, 73
Camp De Wolfe, Wading River, NY, 182
Camp Pioneer (Lutheran), Angola, NY, 179
Camp Epworth, High Falls, NY, 180
Camp Sequanota Enrichment Center, Jennerstown, PA, 200
Campion Renewal Center, Weston, MA, 73
Cardinal Spellman Retreat House, Riverdale, NY, 181
Cardinal Wright Vocation and Prayer Center, Gibsonia, PA, 200
Carlow College Campus Ministry, Pittsburgh, PA, 201
Carmelite Retreat House, Mahwah, NJ, 107
Cenacle Retreat House, Lake Ronkonkoma, NY, 180
Cenacle Retreat House, Brighton, MA, 71
Cenacle Retreat House, Highland Park, NJ, 107
Cenacle Retreat House, Pittsburgh, PA, 201
Cenacle Center for Spiritual Renewal, Rochester, NY, 181
Center for Christian Living, Clarence, NY, 179
Center of Renewal, Stella Niagara, NY, 182
Christ the King Retreat House, Syracuse, NY, 182
Ciotti Manor, Butler, PA, 199
Ciotti Manor, Herman, PA, 200
The Community of Jesus, Inc., Orleans, MA, 72
Community of the Way of the Cross Retreat Center, Buffalo, NY, 179
Convent of St. Helena, Vails Gate, NY, 182
Craigville Conference Center, Craigville, MA, 71
Cursillos Center, Brooklyn, NY, 179
Deer Hill Conference and Retreat Center, Wappingers Falls, NY, 182

Deering Conference Center, Deering, NH, 91
Discovery Jewish Heritage Seminars, New York, NY, 181
Dominican Reflection Center, Ossining, NY, 181
Dominican Retreat House, Schenectady, NY, 182
Ecclesia Center, Gerard, PA, 200
Edmundite Apostolate and Conference Center, Mystic, CT, 23
Emmanuel Christian Church Retreat House, Glenmont, NY, 180
Emmaus Retreat House, Perth Amboy, NJ, 107
Emmaus-Diocesan Spiritual Life Center, Uncasville, CT, 23
Episcopal Camp and Conference Center, ivoryton, CT, 23
Espousal Retreat and Conference Center, Waltham, MA, 73
Esther House of Spiritual Renewal, Worcester, MA, 73
Father Marot CYO Center, Woonsocket, RI, 219
Fatima House, Bedminster, PA, 199
Fatima House, Ottsville, PA, 200
Fatima Renewal Center, Dalton, PA, 199
Fellowship Farm, Pottsdown, PA, 201
Foyer of Charity, North Scituate, MA, 72
Francis House of Prayer, Mount Holly, NJ, 107
Genesis Spiritual Life Center, Wesfield, MA, 73
Geneva Point Center, Center Harbor, NH, 91
Gilmary Diocesan Center, Coraopolis, PA, 199
Grail Conference Center, Cornwall-on-Hudson, NY, 179
Green Hills Methodist Camp, Barree, PA, 199
Grotonwood, Groton, MA, 71
Hadassah "Kallahs," Jewish Education Dept., New York, NY, 181
The Himalayan Institute, Honesdale, PA, 200
Holy Cross Fathers Retreat, North Dartmouth, MA, 72
Holy Cross Fathers Retreat House, North Easton, MA, 72
Holy Family House of Prayer, Rockville Centre, NY, 181
Holy Family Retreat House, West Hartford, CT, 23
Holy Shankaracharya, Stroudsburg, PA, 201
Holy Trinity Monastery, Jordanville, NY, 180
House of Holy Innocents, Mount Sinai, NY, 181
Immaculata Retreat House, Willimantic, CT, 23
Ingraham House, Bristol, CT, 23
Inn of the Spirit, Yulan, NY, 183
Island Retreat, Tupper Lake, NY, 182
Jain Ashram, Blairstown, NJ, 107
Jesuit Center for Spiritual Growth, Wernersville, PA, 201
John Woolman Memorial House, Mount Holly, NJ, 107
Joseph House, Manchester, NH, 91
Kanzeon Zen Center, Bar Harbor, ME, 43
Kirby Episcopal House, Glen Summit, PA, 200
Kirkridge, Bangor, PA, 199
LaSalette Center for Christian Living, Attleboro, MA, 71
LaSalette Retreat Center, Brewster, MA, 71
LaSalette Shrine and Conference Center, Enfield, NH, 91
Laurelville Mennonite Church Center, Mount Pleasant, PA, 200
Lily Dale Metaphysical Assembly, Cassadaga, NY, 179
Little Portion Friary, Mount Sinai, NY, 181
Lutheran Deaconess Community Center, Gladwyne, PA, 200
Mandala Buddhist Center, Lincoln, VT, 231
Marian Center, Inc., Holyoke, MA, 72
Mariandale Dominican Sisters, Ossining, NY, 181
The Marianist, Cape May Point, NJ, 107
Marist Brothers Retreat House, Esopus, NY, 180

The Marist House, Framingham, MA, 71
Mary House, Spencer, MA, 73
Maryknoll Mission Institute, Maryknoll, NY, 180
Matagiri, Mount Tremper, NY, 181
Maycroft, Sag Harbor, NY, 182
Medical Mission Sisters, Philadelphia, PA, 200
Memorial House Center for Spiritual Direction, Springfield, MA, 73
Mercy Consultation Center, Dallas, PA, 199
Metropolitan Baptist Camp, Poughquag, NY, 181
Monastery of Bethlehem, Livingston Manor, NY, 180
Monastery of Mary the Queen, Elmira, NY, 180
Morgan Bay Zendo, Surry, ME, 43
Morningstar House of Prayer, Trenton, NJ, 108
Mother of Sorrows Retreat House, West Springfield, MA, 73
Mount Asbury Methodist Center, Newville, PA, 200
Mount Assisi Monastery, Loretto, PA, 200
Mount Alvernia Retreat House, Wappingers Falls, NY, 182
Mount Alverno Center, Warwick, NY, 182
Mount Eden Retreat, Washington, NJ, 108
Mount Manresa, Staten Island, NY, 182
Mount Marie Conference Center, Holyoke, MA, 72
Mount St. Francis Retreat Center, Ringwood, NJ, 107
Mount St. Macrina Retreat Center, Uniontown, PA, 201
Mount St. Mary Convent, Burlington, VT, 231
My Father's House, Moodus, CT, 23
National Shrine of Our Lady of LaSalette, Ipswich, MA, 72
New England Keswich Youth Camp, Monterey, MA, 72
New York City Mission Society, Dover Plains, NY, 180
Northern Pines, Raymond, ME, 43
Notre Dame Retreat House, Canandaigua, NY, 179
Oblate Retreat House, Hudson, NH, 91
Oceanwood, Ocean Park, ME, 43
Olmstead Manor Adult Retreat Renewal Center, Ludlow, PA, 200
Order of St. Anne, Lincoln, MA, 72
Orthodox Monastery of the Transfiguration, Ellwood City, PA, 200
Osgood Hill Conference Center, North Andover, MA, 72
Our Lady of Calvary Retreat House, Farmington, CT, 23
Our Lady of Hope Center, Newburgh, NY, 181
Our Lady of the Sacred Heart Convent, Coraopolis, PA, 199
Packard Manse, Stoughton, MA, 73
Passionist Retreat and Conference Center, West Springfield, MA, 73
Pathwork Center, Phoenicia, NY, 181
Pioneer Valley Zendo, Charlemont, MA, 71
Powell House, Old Chatham, NY, 181
Precious Blood Convent, Shillington, PA, 201
Precious Blood Spirituality Center, Columbia, PA, 199
Presbyterian Center at Holmes, Holmes, NY, 180
Providence Center, Yardley, PA, 201
Pumpkin Hollow Farm, Craryville, NY, 180
Regina Mundi Priory, Devon, PA, 200
Resurrection House, Saranac Lake, NY, 182
Retreat House, Highland Park, NJ
Rockcraft Lodge, East Sebago, ME, 43
Rolling Ridge Conference Center, North Andover, MA, 72
Rowe Camp and Conference Center, Rowe, MA, 72
Rune Hill, Spencer, NY, 182
Salesian Center for Youth Ministry, Goshen, NY, 180
Salvation Army, Sharon, MA, 72
San Alfonso Retreat House, Long Branch, NJ, 107
San Damiano Center, Aston, PA, 199

Self Realization Fellowship, Shaftesbury, VT
Servants of the Cross, Topsham, ME, 43
Sirius Community, Shutesbury, MA, 72
Sisters of St. Ann, Mount St. Ann Retreat House, Ebensburg, PA, 200
Sisters of St. Joseph Retreat Center, Cohasset, MA, 71
Sisters of the Good Shepard Spiritual Center, Peekskill, NY, 181
Sisters of the Precious Blood, Manchester, NH, 91
Skye Farm Camps, Warrensburg, NY, 182
Society of St. John the Evangelist, Cambridge, MA, 71
Spruce Lake Retreat, Canadensis, PA, 199
St. Andrew's House, Walden, NY, 182
St. Barnabas House Retreat and Conference Center, North East, PA, 200
St. Benedict's House, Camden, ME, 43
St. Columban Center, Derby, NY, 180
St. Dominic Savio Youth Center, Peacedale, RI, 219
St. Emma Retreat House, Greensburg, PA, 200
St. Francis Center for Renewal, Bethlehem, PA, 199
St. Francis Friary Retreat House, Easton, PA, 200
St. Francis Retreat House, Fonda, NY, 180
St. Gabriel's Retreat House, Clarks Summit, PA, 199
St. Ignatius Renewal Center, Clarence Center, NY, 179
St. Ignatius Retreat House, Manhasset, NY, 180
St. Joseph by the Sea, South Mantoloking, NJ, 107
St. Joseph's Convent, North Brookfield, MA, 72
St. Joseph's Convent, Webster, MA, 73
St. Joseph's Cursillo Center, New York, NY, 181
St. Joseph's Hall, North Dartmouth, MA, 72
St. Joseph's Villa, Peapack, NJ, 107
St. Margaret's Convent, Boston, MA, 71
St. Margaret's Convent, Duxbury, MA, 71
St. Margaret's House, New Hartford, NY, 181
St. Margaret's House, Philadelphia, PA, 201
St. Mary's Convent and Retreat House, Plattsburgh, NY, 181
St. Mary's House of Greater Solitude, Bedford, PA, 199
St. Mary's Mission Center, Champlain, NY, 179
St. Paul's Center, Brooklyn, NY, 179
St. Paul's Retreat House and Cursillo Center, Augusta, ME, 43
St. Paul's Retreat House, Pittsburgh, PA, 201
St. Pius X House, Blackwood, NJ, 107
St. Scholastica, Petersham, MA, 72
St. Ursula Center, Blue Point, NY, 179
St. Vincent Summer Retreat House, Latrobe, PA, 200
Stella Maris Retreat Center, Skaneateles, NY, 182
Stella Maris Retreat House, Elberon, NJ, 107
Stony Point Center, Stony Point, NY, 182
Stump Sprouts Lodge, West Hawley, MA, 73
SYDA Foundation, South Fallsburg, NY, 182
Temenos, Shutesbury, MA, 72
Thornfield Conference Center, Cazenovia, NY, 179
Tibetan Buddhist Learning Center, Washington, NJ, 108
Trinita Ecumenical Center, New Hartford, CT, 23
Trinity Center, Stirling, NJ, 107
Trinity Retreat, Larchmont, NY, 180
Trinity Spiritual Center, Camp Hill, PA, 199
Unirondack, Inc., Lowville, NY, 180
United Church of Christ Conference Center, Framingham, MA, 71
The Upper Room Spiritual Center, Neptune, NJ, 107
Vanderkamp, Cleveland, NY, 179

Villa Maria by the Sea Retreat House, Stone Harbor, NJ, 108
Villa Maria Community Center, Villa Maria, PA, 201
Villa of Our Lady Retreat House, Mount Pocono, PA, 200
Vipassana Meditation Center, Shelburne Falls, MA, 72
Wainwright House, Rye, NY, 182
Warwick Conference Center, Warwick, NY, 182
Watson Homestead Conference and Retreat Center, Painted Post, NY, 181
Wilbur Herrlich Retreat Center, Holmes, NY, 180
Wise Woman Center, Woodstock, NY, 183
Xavier Center, Convent Station, NJ, 107

About the Authors

Jack and Marcia Kelly are writers who live in New York City. Over the years they have chosen monasteries and retreats as stopping places in their travels. This book is a result of those happy sojourns.